Fundamentals of Municipal Bonds

Fundamentals of Municipal Bonds

Public Securities Association

Revised Edition

PSA

New York

Revised Edition

© 1981, 1982 by Public Securities Association

Library of Congress Catalog Card Number: 80-83540

ISBN 0-9605198-0-7

Printed in the United States of America

Contents

v

Figures

Contents

Preface

Fundamentals of Municipal Bonds has long been regarded as a definitive and informative basic text on the municipal securities market. It was first published under the auspices of the Investment Bankers Association (IBA) and was last updated and reprinted in 1973 by the Securities Industry Association (SIA) through the efforts of the Public Finance Information and Education Committee of the SIA.

The Public Securities Association (PSA) was established in 1977 to continue the work of the IBA and the SIA in serving the members of the public securities industry. PSA currently has nearly 300 dealer and dealer bank members that underwrite, trade, and sell securities issued by state and local governments and securities of the U.S. Government and its agencies. In 1980, PSA members underwrote more than 95 percent of new issues of municipal securities. The Association also has 85 associate members who are affiliated with the public securities markets.

In recognition of the many new developments in the municipal securities market in recent years, PSA has produced an entirely new *Fundamentals of Municipal Bonds*. This text is intended to provide a basic understanding of the municipal securities market to:

1. newcomers to the municipal securities industry who are preparing for a professional qualifications examination;
2. other securities industry professionals who seek to increase their knowledge of the municipal market to serve their clients and customers better;
3. individuals engaged in portfolio management for institutional investors;
4. public officials who wish to understand better the capital-raising mechanism for state and local governments;
5. individual investors, academicians, and students seeking an overview of the municipal securities market.

Many individual participants and organizations in the municipal securities market deserve recognition for their contributions to the preparation of this text. Interviews with industry members provided an important source of knowledge. Among those interviewed were Richard J. Ackermann and Norman I. Schvey, Merrill Lynch White Weld Capital Markets Group; Albert F. Blaylock, United California Bank; Lloyd A. Bush, Lloyd Bush and Associates; Robert J. Butler, Kemper Financial Services; W. J. Turner L. Cobden, and George D. Friedlander, Smith Barney, Harris Upham & Co., Inc.; Philip M. Dearborn, The Greater Washington Research Center; Robert N. Downey, Frank F. Martin and Garland E. Wood, Goldman, Sachs & Co.; Donald J. Robinson and James R. Eustis, Hawkins, Delafield & Wood; Ralph H. Gibbon, Richard K. Desmond, John D. Cummins, and Robert W. Doty and staff, Squire, Sanders & Dempsey; Philip W. Goldsmith, Prescott, Ball & Turben; Gilman C. Gunn III, Park, Ryan, Inc.; Brenton W. Harries and staff, Standard & Poor's Corporation; Donald R. Hodgman, O'Melveny & Myers; Alois S. Jurcik, Morgan Guaranty Trust Company of New York; George Kaufman and Michael Hopewell, Center for Capital Market Research, University of Oregon; J. Kevin Kenny and Staff, J. J. Kenny Co., Inc.; James A. Lebenthal, Lebenthal & Co., Inc.; Alan C. Lerner and Paul D. Muller, Bankers Trust Company; John J. Lynch, Jr., J. F. Hartfield & Co., Inc.; Lauren M. Miralia, Municipal Bond Insurance Association; John J. O'Brien, and Philip M. Law, Jr., and staff, Salomon Brothers; John E. Petersen, Government Finance Research Center/ Municipal Finance Officers Association; the late Jackson R. E. Phillips, Moody's Investors Service; Scott Pierce and Robert A. Meyer, E. F. Hutton & Co., Inc.; David R. Rochat, Donaldson, Lufkin & Jenrette Securities Corporation; Stanley D. Rosenberg, Munifacts Newswire Services; Bernard L. Smith, Jr., and Arthur E. Schloss, The First Boston Corporation; Larry D. Sobel, Ballard, Spahr, Andrews & Ingersoll; Harold I. Steinberg, Peat, Marwick, Mitchell & Co.; Christopher A. Taylor and Donald F. Donahue, Municipal Securities Rulemaking Board; David G. Taylor and Gordon E. McDanold and staff, Continental Illinois National Bank and Trust Company of Chicago; Peter C. Trent, Shearson Loeb Rhoades Inc.; Richard C. Trepp, Richard C. Trepp & Company; and Kenneth R. Von der Heiden, Kidder, Peabody & Co., Incorporated.

In addition, an industry review committee assisted in editing the text. Participants in this committee were: Eleanor Lebenthal Bissinger, Lebenthal & Co., Inc.; George W. Benoit, Matthews & Wright, Inc.; Albert F. Blaylock, United California Bank; Walter R. Chambers, The

Ohio Company; E. George Cross III, Philadelphia National Bank; John D. Cummins, Esq., Squire, Sanders & Dempsey; J. Kevin Kenny, J. J. Kenny Co., Inc.; Robert R. Martin, Dain Bosworth, Incorporated; Frank O'Brien, J. F. Hartfield & Co., Inc.; Donald J. Robinson, Esq., Hawkins, Delafield & Wood; David R. Rochat, Donaldson, Lufkin & Jenrette Securities Corporation; Jean J. Rousseau, Merrill Lynch, Pierce, Fenner & Smith Inc.; John F. Thompson, W. H. Morton & Co.; Peter C. Trent, Shearson Loeb Rhoades Inc.; Karl H. Velde, Jr., William Blair & Company.

Financial writer Jeffrey G. Madrick was the principal author of the text. Also contributing to the preparation and editing of the material were members of the PSA staff, particularly Executive Director Arthur J. Kalita and Director of Communications Caroline M. Benn, and Roger Klein, past Executive Director of PSA.

LAWRENCE H. BROWN
Chairman
Public Securities Association,
1979-1980

FUNDAMENTALS OF MUNICIPAL BONDS

Introduction: A Decade of Change in the Municipal Securities Industry

The debt of state and local governments has grown rapidly, with only a handful of interruptions, for more than a century and a half. Debt financing became an acceptable means to support the development of the young, vigorous cities in the 1820s. The amount of state and local debt outstanding expanded quickly during the remainder of the century, set back seriously only by the Panic of 1873 and its aftermath. In the year 1900, state and local governments borrowed $175 million from investors, bringing the level of outstanding debt to more than $2 billion.

In the twentieth century, the volume of offerings continued to push upward. Total state and local debt outstanding had reached $5 billion when the Sixteenth Amendment to the United States Constitution established the Federal income tax in 1913. Interest on state and local issues was exempted from the new tax and, as a result, yields fell markedly compared to rates on taxable corporate and U.S. government securities. Only in the last years of the Depression and during World War II did growth in volume stop altogether. By 1950, there were about $24 billion of outstanding *municipal* securities—a term that by convention has come to include all publicly-offered state and local debt. In 1960, new issues totaled $11 billion and the amount outstanding exceeded $70 billion. (See Figure I-1.)

Events of the 1960s and especially the 1970s, however, were to make the municipal markets of most former decades seem dull by comparison. The growth of the market was remarkable, a sixfold increase between 1960 and 1980. The volume of new issues in 1980 alone was $76 billion—

1

FIGURE I-1.   State and Local Debt Outstanding, 1945-1980

(In Millions of Dollars)

1980	$325,516	1962	81,209
1979	312,793	1961	75,851
1978	291,438	1960	70,766
1977	263,160	1959	65,486
1976	239,507	1958	59,206
1975	223,843	1957	53,708
1974	207,695	1956	49,461
1973	191,215	1955	45,870
1972	176,507	1954	40,594
1971	161,798	1953	34,512
1970	144,376	1952	30,243
1969	133,145	1951	26,559
1968	123,219	1950	24,381
1967	113,703	1949	21,049
1966	105,925	1948	18,467
1965	100,278	1947	16,298
1964	92,933	1946	14,886
1963	86,932	1945	14,818

SOURCE: Federal Reserve Board

exceeding the total amount outstanding in 1961. One reason was the rapid expansion of short-term debt. The use of short-term debt by municipalities to provide funds prior to and in anticipation of tax collections and other revenues has become a conventional financing technique. The annual volume of short-term borrowing rose from only $4 billion in 1960 to $27.7 billion in 1980. (See Figure I-2.)

The most far-reaching change in the municipal marketplace has been the rise and eventual domination of the market by revenue bonds. Traditional municipal debt had been issued over the years primarily as a general obligation of the state or local government. General obligation bonds are backed by the "full faith and credit" of the issuer—in other words the full taxing power of the state or local government. Revenue bonds, on the other hand, usually have no claim on the other revenues of the issuer. Rather, they are issued to support a particular project, such as a utility, and they are typically paid for out of the revenues generated by that project. By the end of the 1970s, the volume of new revenue bonds was outpacing traditional

FIGURE I-2. State and Local Borrowing, 1960-1980

Volume of New Issues of Long- and Short-Term Securities

Year	Long-Term	Short-Term	Total	Total Number
1980	$48,367,802,000	$27,719,623,000	$76,087,425,000	7,933
1979	43,308,907,000	21,709,280,000	65,018,187,000	7,453
1978	48,348,957,000	21,383,806,000	69,732,763,000	8,066
1977	46,705,886,000	24,750,851,000	71,456,737,000	8,333
1976	35,313,601,000	20,078,713,000	55,392,314,000	6,932
1975	29,326,229,546	28,972,825,923	58,299,055,469	8,107
1974	22,823,968,194	29,040,681,526	51,864,649,720	7,701
1973	22,952,646,766	24,667,357,290	47,620,004,056	8,147
1972	22,940,843,384	25,221,768,335	49,162,611,719	8,420
1971	24,369,536,105	26,281,467,539	50,651,003,644	8,811
1970	17,761,645,833	17,879,952,793	35,641,598,626	7,604
1969	11,460,251,103	11,783,127,124	23,243,378,227	6,395
1968	16,374,332,960	8,658,556,650	25,032,889,610	7,887
1967	14,287,949,346	8,025,331,071	22,313,280,417	7,964
1966	11,088,938,349	6,523,534,545	17,612,472,894	7,430
1965	11,084,188,715	6,537,396,751	17,621,585,466	7,977
1964	10,544,127,114	5,423,258,660	15,967,385,774	8,138
1963	10,106,665,364	5,480,807,517	15,587,472,881	8,574
1962	8,558,200,662	4,763,474,695	13,321,675,357	8,689
1961	8,359,512,134	4,514,171,800	12,873,683,934	8,490
1960	7,229,500,359	4,006,185,985	11,235,686,344	8,397

SOURCE: Public Securities Association Municipal Securities Data Base; The Bond Buyer's Municipal Finance Statistics, 1960-1975

general obligation debt by almost a two-to-one margin. Only a decade earlier, general obligation debt comprised some 65 percent of annual new issues.

With revenue bonds, municipalities have been able to expand their uses of tax-exempt borrowing. Indeed, municipal debt has increasingly been used to support various public purpose projects once financed only by the private sector. In the 1950s, revenue bonds were issued primarily for highways, turnpikes, and public utilities. By the 1970s, tax-exempt revenue bonds were being issued to provide financing for housing, hospitals, industrial pollution control equipment, massive public power projects sometimes involving several public and private utilities, and sports stadiums and convention centers. A hybrid bond of sorts, the moral obligation bond also became a popular, if controversial, method of financing some state projects. These bonds are secured by revenues from the project. In addition, they are secured by a moral though not binding obligation on the part of the state to make up any shortfall in debt service reserve funds.

The municipal bond market was also to be tested by some disruptions in the 1970s. Few occurrences in the history of the municipal securities market were more momentous than New York City's financial difficulties in 1975. After rapidly increasing its outstanding debt for more than a decade, New York City's access to the municipal securities market came to an abrupt halt. The City defaulted on a note issue and prices of some outstanding City obligations declined substantially. New York City's problems, in turn, cast doubt on the security of various municipal credits throughout the country.

Still, for investors in municipal bonds, the temporary note default by New York City came as a sudden jolt. The rating agencies, Moody's Investors Service Inc. and Standard & Poor's Corporation, had given New York City bonds a respectable rating of A prior to 1975. Municipal issues, long considered in safety second only to U.S. government securities, suddenly acquired an element of serious risk.

For all its drama, however, New York City's crisis actually had less long-term impact on the market than events that occurred earlier in the decade. Until the 1970s, the municipal securities industry had not been subject to any direct Federal securities regulation, having been exempted from the Securities Acts of 1933 and 1934, which established regulation for other securities markets. But a number of proceedings initiated by the Securities and Exchange Commission against several dealers in municipal securities captured the attention of Congress and a demand for some form of regulation arose. In 1975, Congress passed Securities Acts Amendments that established the Municipal Securities Rulemaking Board (MSRB), composed of industry and public members, to write rules governing the activities of brokers and dealers in the municipal securities market. The 1975 Amendments also required all municipal securities dealers and brokers to register with the Securities and Exchange Commission and the MSRB to establish qualifications examinations for municipal securities professionals.

By 1979, the MSRB had written the bulk of its regulations. However, there were demands in Congress for greater Federal involvement in the municipal securities market. Two major concerns were the disclosure of information by issuers on new issues of municipal securities and the accounting and financial reporting practices of state and local governments. Issues of corporate securities are subject to a review by the Securities and Exchange Commission, but municipal issuers are still exempt from this Federal involvement. Other areas that have aroused Federal interest are the funding of municipal pension funds, the investment of proceeds of municipal bond issues, and some of the newer uses of tax-exempt financing that some Federal officials believe stretch the "public purpose" to which tax-exempt financing is restricted.

In the latter half of the 1970s, the municipal bond market regained its equilibrium, and most industry observers readily agree that the municipal marketplace is stronger than it was earlier in the decade. What is certainly clear is that the market is far different from what it was only a decade earlier. New kinds of bonds providing financing for an expanding spectrum of public purposes became common. State and local governments improved their financial management and increased their disclosure of information. The rating agencies markedly bolstered their operations. Underwriters became more sophisticated, imaginative, and, indeed, competitive. The role of bond counsel broadened considerably.

Such rapid and sweeping change has left a gap in the basic literature on the municipal securities industry. This volume is intended to help fill that gap. It is a fundamental text for any individual interested in acquiring an understanding of the basics of the municipal securities market and provides a broad and up-to-date summary of all important principles and practices in the industry. Its range is intentionally very wide. Specialists will find it a valuable guide to those areas of the business outside their own fields. The newcomer to the industry will find it an accessible, clear, and accurate primer that covers the important basic information about the securities and the industry. It may be particularly helpful to those preparing for the MSRB qualifications examinations.

The first chapter covers the rudimentary characteristics and technicalities of municipal securities, and defines the various important types of bonds. Chapter 2 outlines the roles of all the major participants in the market, from issuers to investors. The objective is to give the reader an overview of the entire marketplace and the functions performed by the various market participants. Several of the major participants, however, require their own chapters. Chapters 3, 4, and 5 discuss in greater depth the issuers, underwriters, and the secondary market, respectively. The roles of dealers as underwriter and market maker are examined carefully in the latter two chapters.

The major investors are discussed in Chapter 6, as are basic investing strategies and tax matters that affect investors. In Chapter 7, what analysts look for in determining the credit worthiness of general obligation and revenue bonds is examined. The economic, financial, and special market factors that determine the level of municipal interest rates are the subject of Chapter 8. Chapter 9 includes a summary of the current rules of the Municipal Securities Rulemaking Board, as well as a look at other areas of Federal oversight and involvement in the municipal securities market. The historical basis for the tax exemption is also discussed. The Appendix on mathematical calculations reviews both the theory and the methods of calculating yields and bids.

The Basics of Municipal Securities

The Tax Exemption

The characteristic that sets municipal securities apart from all other securities is the tax exemption. The interest income on municipal bonds has always been exempt from Federal income tax. Local issues are usually exempted from state tax in their own states as well, although states generally tax the interest income from the securities of other states. Proponents argue that there is a strong constitutional basis for the Federal exemption. The argument rests on the reciprocal immunity doctrine under the U.S. Constitution, which holds that states cannot interfere in the affairs of the Federal government, and the Federal government cannot interfere in state affairs. When the income tax law was passed, this doctrine prevailed and a clause was written into the Internal Revenue Code clearly stating that interest on municipal securities was exempt (Chapter 9). Today, Section 103 of the Internal Revenue Code of 1954 provides the statutory exemption from taxation of interest on municipal securities.

The savings that the tax exemption brings state and local issuers became obvious soon after the first Federal income tax was initiated. Before 1913, interest rates on municipal securities were about the same as rates on corporate bonds. After 1913, the rates on the tax-exempt securities fell sharply in relation to taxable corporate bond interest rates. Through most of the 1970s, interest rates for long-term municipal

7

FIGURE 1-1.   Municipal Bond Yields as a Percentage of Corporate Yields, 1970-1980

Year	Average Aa Municipal Yield*	÷ Average Aa Corporate Yield*	= % Ratio
1970	6.28	8.32	75
1971	5.36	7.78	69
1972	5.19	7.48	69
1973	5.09	7.66	66
1974	6.04	8.84	68
1975	6.77	9.17	74
1976	6.12	8.75	70
1977	5.39	8.24	65
1978	5.68	8.92	63
1979	6.12	9.94	61
1980	8.06	12.50	64

SOURCE: Moody's Bond Survey. Percentage calculations prepared by Public Securities Association.

*Moody's yearly averages of yields on Aa municipal and Aa corporate bonds.

State and local governments achieve considerable interest cost savings in debt financing as a result of the tax-exempt status of municipal bonds. In 1980, interest rates on long-term municipal bonds averaged 35% lower than rates on comparable corporate securities.

securities have averaged around 65 percent to 70 percent of rates on comparable long-term corporate bonds. (See Figure 1-1.)

Investors are willing to receive the lower yields because of the tax exemption. Just how advantageous the tax exemption is depends on the taxpayer's bracket. A quality long-term municipal bond in 1980 was paying an interest rate of 8.45 percent a year. To an unmarried investor in the 49 percent Federal income tax bracket, that 8.45 percent a year tax-free is the equivalent of a 16.57 percent return on a taxable bond. In other words, almost half of the interest on an equivalent corporate bond would have gone to pay Federal income tax. A single investor in the 30 percent tax bracket would have to earn 12.07 percent on a corporate bond to earn the same return. By comparison, a comparable corporate bond in 1980 was paying 12.89 percent. (See Figure 1-2.)

The relative advantage of tax-exempt bonds is greater in states which have state and local income taxes, for those bonds which are exempt from the state and local taxes as well. While laws vary greatly from state to state, many states exempt only interest income on bonds issued within their state. An unmarried New York City resident in the 49% Federal tax bracket would also generally be subject to a 14% State tax and a 4.3% City tax. It should be noted, however, that taxes paid on State and Local income tax returns are deductible on the Federal return. Assuming that the investor itemizes deductions, the effect of the State tax must therefore be adjusted by the amount gained back from the deduction on the Federal return. The total effective income tax rate for that individual is thus not 49% + 14% + 4.3% = 67.3% but 49% + 14% (1−.49) + 4.3% (1−.49), or 58.3%. A 9% return on a municipal bond for that New York City resident thus has the same after-tax benefit as a 21.6% taxable bond, since (21.6%) (1−.583) = 9%.

The Taxable Yield Equivalent Formula

The computation of these taxable yield equivalents is shown below. They are the industry's standard way of demonstrating to investors the relative advantages of tax-exempt bonds. An important point to remember is that the taxpayer's marginal tax rate is the relevant bracket for computing the equivalent yield. Federal income tax rates increase with each additional few thousand dollars earned. The marginal tax rate is that rate which would be applied to any additional money earned. For example, a married couple filing a joint return would pay taxes of 33 percent on that portion of a taxable income above about $30,000 a year and below about $35,000. The Federal rate on taxable income above $35,000 but below $46,000 is 39 percent. This is the marginal rate. Thus, a couple earning $35,000 in salary and $1,000 in interest on a taxable bond will pay $390 in tax on the additional $1,000 of income. This couple would have to earn only $610 of interest on a tax-exempt bond to do as well. A simple formula follows that calculates just what yield would have to be earned on a taxable bond to equal the yield being earned on a tax-free municipal bond.

$$\frac{\text{Tax-free yield}}{100\% - \text{marginal tax bracket}} = \text{taxable yield equivalent}$$

For the couple, then, that earns $35,000 a year and has bought a municipal bond yielding 7 percent, the taxable yield equivalent is 11.5 percent.

$$\frac{7\%}{100\% - 39\%} = \frac{7\%}{61\%} = 11.5\%$$

FIGURE 1-2. Tax-Exempt/Taxable Yield Equivalent Tables

- Select the appropriate return (single or joint return).
- Determine which tax bracket you are in according to the amount of taxable income you have. Taxable income is your income after the appropriate exemptions and deductions are taken. (The tables do not take into account special provisions affecting Federal tax rates, especially the maximum and minimum taxes.)
- The numbers in the column under your tax bracket give you the approximate taxable yield equivalent for each of the tax-exempt yields in the far left column.

SINGLE RETURN

Taxable Income in Thousands	$18.2 to $23.5	$23.5 to $28.8	$28.8 to $34.1	$39.1 to $41.5	over $41.5
% Tax Bracket	31	35	40	44	50
6.0	8.7	9.2	10.0	10.7	12.0
7.0	10.1	10.8	11.7	12.5	14.0
7.5	10.9	11.5	12.5	13.4	15.0
8.0	11.6	12.3	13.3	14.3	16.0
8.5	12.3	13.1	14.2	15.2	17.0
9.0	13.0	13.8	15.0	16.1	18.0
9.5	13.8	14.6	15.8	17.0	19.0
10.0	14.5	15.4	16.7	17.9	20.0
10.5	15.2	16.2	17.5	18.8	21.0
11.0	15.9	16.9	18.3	19.6	22.0
11.5	16.7	17.7	19.2	20.5	23.0
12.0	17.4	18.5	20.0	21.4	24.0
12.5	18.1	19.2	20.8	22.3	25.0
13.0	18.8	20.0	21.7	23.2	26.0
13.5	19.6	20.8	22.5	24.1	27.0
14.0	20.3	21.5	23.3	25.0	28.0
14.5	21.0	22.3	24.2	25.9	29.0
15.0	21.7	23.1	25.0	26.8	30.0
16.0	23.2	24.6	26.7	28.6	32.0

Tax-Exempt Yields (%) (left axis label)

JOINT RETURN

Taxable Income in Thousands	$24.6 to $29.9	$29.9 to $35.2	$35.2 to $45.8	$45.8 to $60.0	$60.0 to $85.6	over $85.6
% Tax Bracket	29	33	39	44	49	50
6.0	8.5	9.0	9.8	10.7	11.8	12.0
7.0	9.9	10.4	11.5	12.5	13.7	14.0
7.5	10.6	11.2	12.3	13.4	14.7	15.0
8.0	11.3	11.9	13.1	14.3	15.7	16.0
8.5	12.0	12.7	13.9	15.2	16.7	17.0
9.0	12.7	13.4	14.8	16.1	17.6	18.0
9.5	13.4	14.2	15.6	17.0	18.6	19.0
10.0	14.1	14.9	16.4	17.9	19.6	20.0
10.5	14.8	15.7	17.2	18.8	20.6	21.0
11.0	15.5	16.4	18.0	19.6	21.6	22.0
11.5	16.2	17.2	18.9	20.5	22.5	23.0
12.0	16.9	17.9	19.7	21.4	23.5	24.0
12.5	17.6	18.7	20.5	22.3	24.5	25.0
13.0	18.3	19.4	21.3	23.2	25.5	26.0
13.5	19.0	20.1	22.1	24.1	26.5	27.0
14.0	19.7	20.9	23.0	25.0	27.5	28.0
14.5	20.4	21.6	23.8	25.9	28.4	29.0
15.0	21.1	22.4	24.6	26.8	29.4	30.0
16.0	22.5	23.9	26.2	28.6	31.4	32.0

Tax-Exempt Yields (%)

Description of a Municipal Bond

Municipal bonds are usually issued in denominations of $5,000, known as the par value or face value amount of the bond. That is the amount, or principal, paid when the bonds mature. Up to the 1960s, the conventional denomination was $1,000, and terminology is still based on the $1,000 bond. When a dealer says "one bond," he or she is referring to $1,000 par value. "Twenty-five bonds" are $25,000 par value, although there may be only five bond certificates in denominations of $5,000 each. In recent years, several municipalities have experimented with denominations as low as $100 to try to attract smaller investors, but the practice has not become widespread.

Any particular municipal bond, like most other bonds, is identified by four pieces of information.

1. *Name of the issuer.* The issuing body, of course, is the first essential piece of information.

2. *Coupon.* This is the interest rate that is stated on the bond and that is payable to the bondholder. The dollar amount paid is fixed over the life of the bonds. Interest on municipal bonds is usually paid semiannually. Thus, a $1,000 bond with a coupon rate of 6 percent will pay $60 a year to the bondholder, $30 every six months.

3. *Maturity date.* This is the date on which the investor will receive payment of principal and the final interest payment. In other words, it is the day, month, and year that the bondholder will receive the $1,000 par value of the bond.

4. *Yield (or price).* Corporate and U.S. government bonds are generally quoted in terms of price, but municipal bonds are generally quoted in terms of yield because there are so many issues of different maturities. Since the coupon interest payment is fixed, the price of a bond must change in order to keep the yield in line with other newly issued bonds. Bond prices are stated as a percentage of the par value. Par value equals 100; a discount bond trades at a price below 100, say, 97, or $970 for a bond with a par value of $1,000; a premium bond trades at a price above 100, say, 102, or $1,020 for a bond with a $1,000 par value.

When the price changes, the yield must also change. An investor who pays less than par for a bond with a 6 percent coupon is receiving more than 6 percent in yield. In other words, the investor is receiving $60 of interest each year for an investment of less than $1,000. An investor who pays more than par receives a yield of less than 6 percent. Yields on municipal bonds are usually quoted in increments of 0.05 percent or 5 basis points (a "basis point" is equal to 1/100 of 1 percent).

All bonds are identified by these four pieces of information. A typical municipal bond quotation is as follows: "$10,000 State of Maryland, 5 percent of April 1, 1983, at 5.75 percent." These are $10,000 par value of bonds issued by Maryland with a coupon of 5 percent and maturing on April 1, 1983. They are trading at a price to yield 5.75 percent, which means the price is approximately 98.

Municipal bonds fluctuate in yield for the same economic reasons that other bonds do (Chapter 8). General shifts in interest rates due to Federal Reserve monetary policy or changing expectations about inflation, for example, affect municipal interest rates as well as other interest rates. Short-term swings in the demand for municipal bonds by investors will also affect municipal interest rates. The credit worthiness of a particular issuer could change, causing a shift in yield. As in all bond markets, yields for older issues will rise and fall in line with yields on new issues with similar maturities and risk characteristics.

This is an important concept. A bond issued in the late 1960s may have carried a coupon of 4.5 percent with a sixteen-year maturity. Six years later, a new bond of similar risk with a ten-year maturity may have carried a coupon of 6.5 percent. Both bonds will mature in ten years, so the bond with a coupon of 4.5 percent must fall in price so that its yield will approximate the one on the new 6.5 percent bond. Investors would sell the older bond until its price dropped to 85, not taking all taxes into consideration, in order to push the yield up to a level equivalent to the new bond.

Yield to Maturity

There are several types of yields that can be calculated for different purposes. The current yield, for example, is a quick and simple method to calculate current income on a bond earned from interest payments. The current yield is equal to the coupon interest payment divided by the current price of the bond.

But the yield that is used to identify bonds trading in the market is the yield to maturity, a concept that takes into account the time value of money. If an investor buys a bond at a discount and holds it to maturity, for example, the gain earned at maturity raises the yield to the investor. But that gain received ten years from now is not worth as much as it would be if received today. At the least, it would earn interest income over the ten years if received and invested today. The yield to maturity takes these time considerations into account. In simplest terms, it is the annual return, compounded semiannually, that the investor will earn from all interest and principal payments over the life of the bond. (One important assumption in yield to maturity calculations is that interest payments are reinvested at the yield to maturity.)

The yield to maturity of a bond with a 6 percent coupon bought at par is 6 percent. If the bond is bought at a discount or premium, however, the calculation gets more complicated. If that 6 percent bond had been bought at 90 ($900), and was due in ten years, the yield to maturity would be 7.50 percent. The current yield is 6.67 percent ($60 ÷ $900). Another way to look at the yield to maturity is to use the analogy of a savings account. The investor deposits $900 in the savings account and receives $30 every six months in interest. He or she withdraws $1,000 at the end of ten years. The annual interest return, compounded semiannually, on the account is 7.50 percent— the yield to maturity.

The development of the bond desk calculator has made finding yields to maturity merely a matter of pushing buttons. The Appendix contains a fuller discussion of the theory and computation of the yield to maturity. Before the advanced calculators, the quick way to find yields and prices was with a basis book. An excerpt from a basis book is reproduced in Figure 1-3. By knowing the yield to maturity, the coupon and the maturity of the bond, one would merely look down the table to find the price. Alternatively, if the price is known, the yield to maturity can easily be found by looking across. As long as any three factors are known, the fourth can be found. In the table, a bond due in 12 years with a 5 percent coupon and trading at a yield to maturity of 6.50 percent will have a price of 87.63. (See Figure 1-3.)

Any capital gains earned by selling municipal bonds at a higher price, or redeeming bonds at par that were bought at a discount, are subject to normal capital gains taxes. This will alter the yield to maturity after taxes and also affect the way the bonds are priced in the market. Capital gains taxes are discussed more fully in Chapters 6

FIGURE 1-3. Excerpt from a Basis Book

To use the table:

a. If the maturity of the bond, coupon, and yield to maturity are known, read the corresponding price in the intersecting column.

b. If the price is known, to find the yield to maturity, read across to the left to the appropriate bond yield column.

5%			YEARS and MONTHS				
Yield	10-6	11-0	11-6	12-0	12-6	13-0	13-6	14-0
2.00	128.29	129.49	130.68	131.87	133.03	134.19	135.34	136.47
2.20	126.12	127.22	128.31	129.39	130.45	131.51	132.55	133.58
2.40	124.01	125.01	125.99	126.97	127.93	128.89	129.63	130.76
2.60	121.93	122.83	123.72	124.60	125.47	126.33	127.18	128.01
2.80	119.89	120.70	121.50	122.29	123.07	123.83	124.59	125.34
3.00	117.90	118.62	119.33	120.03	120.72	121.40	122.07	122.73
3.20	115.95	116.58	117.20	117.82	118.42	119.02	119.61	120.18
3.40	114.03	114.58	115.12	115.66	116.18	116.70	117.21	117.71
3.60	112.15	112.62	113.09	113.54	113.99	114.43	114.87	115.29
3.80	110.31	110.71	111.10	111.48	111.85	112.22	112.58	112.94
4.00	108.51	108.83	109.15	109.46	109.76	110.06	110.35	110.64
4.20	106.74	106.99	107.24	107.48	107.72	107.95	108.18	108.40
4.40	105.00	105.19	105.37	105.55	105.72	105.89	106.06	106.22
4.60	103.30	103.42	103.54	103.66	103.77	103.88	103.99	104.10
4.80	101.63	101.69	101.75	101.81	101.86	101.92	101.97	102.02
5.00	100.00	100.00	100.00	100.00	100.00	100.00	100.00	100.00
5.10	99.19	99.17	99.14	99.11	99.08	99.06	99.03	99.01
5.20	98.40	98.34	98.29	98.23	98.18	98.13	98.08	98.03
5.30	97.61	97.52	97.44	97.36	97.28	97.21	97.13	97.06
5.40	96.83	96.71	96.61	96.50	96.40	96.30	96.20	96.11
5.50	96.05	95.91	95.78	95.65	95.52	95.40	95.28	95.16
5.60	95.29	95.12	94.96	94.81	94.66	94.51	94.37	94.23
5.70	94.53	94.34	94.15	93.98	93.80	93.63	93.47	93.31
5.80	93.77	93.56	93.35	93.15	92.96	92.77	92.58	92.40
5.90	93.03	92.79	92.56	92.34	92.12	91.91	91.70	91.50
6.00	92.29	92.03	91.78	91.53	91.29	91.06	90.84	90.62
6.10	91.56	91.28	91.00	90.74	90.48	90.22	89.98	89.74
6.20	90.84	90.53	90.24	89.95	89.67	89.40	89.13	88.88
6.30	90.12	89.79	89.48	89.17	88.87	88.58	88.30	88.02
6.40	89.41	89.06	88.73	88.40	88.08	87.77	87.47	87.18
6.50	88.71	88.34	87.98	87.63	87.30	86.97	86.65	86.35
6.60	88.02	87.63	87.25	86.88	86.52	86.18	85.85	85.52
6.70	87.33	86.92	86.52	86.13	85.76	85.40	85.05	84.71
6.80	86.65	86.22	85.80	85.39	85.00	84.63	84.26	83.91
6.90	85.97	85.52	85.09	84.66	84.26	83.86	83.48	83.12
7.00	85.30	84.83	84.38	83.94	83.52	83.11	82.71	82.33
7.10	84.64	84.15	83.68	83.23	82.79	82.36	81.95	81.56
7.20	83.98	83.48	82.99	82.52	82.07	81.63	81.20	80.79
7.30	83.33	82.81	82.31	81.82	81.35	80.90	80.46	80.04
7.40	82.69	82.15	81.63	81.13	80.64	80.18	79.73	79.29
7.50	82.05	81.50	80.96	80.44	79.95	79.47	79.00	78.56
7.60	81.42	80.85	80.30	79.77	79.26	78.76	78.29	77.83
7.70	80.80	80.21	79.64	79.10	78.57	78.07	77.58	77.11
7.80	80.18	79.57	78.99	78.43	77.90	77.38	76.88	76.40
7.90	79.56	78.95	78.35	77.78	77.23	76.70	76.19	75.70
8.00	78.96	78.32	77.71	77.13	76.57	76.03	75.51	75.01
8.10	78.35	77.71	77.09	76.49	75.91	75.36	74.83	74.32
8.20	77.76	77.10	76.46	75.85	75.27	74.70	74.16	73.64
8.30	77.17	76.49	75.85	75.22	74.63	74.05	73.50	72.98
8.40	76.58	75.90	75.24	74.60	74.00	73.41	72.85	72.31
8.50	76.00	75.30	74.63	73.99	73.37	72.78	72.21	71.66
8.60	75.43	74.72	74.03	73.38	72.75	72.15	71.57	71.02
8.70	74.86	74.14	73.44	72.78	72.14	71.53	70.94	70.38
8.80	74.30	73.56	72.86	72.18	71.53	70.91	70.32	69.75
8.90	73.74	72.99	72.28	71.59	70.94	70.31	69.71	69.13
9.00	73.19	72.43	71.70	71.01	70.34	69.71	69.10	68.51
9.20	72.10	71.32	70.57	69.86	69.18	68.53	67.90	67.31
9.40	71.03	70.23	69.47	68.74	68.04	67.37	66.74	66.13
9.60	69.99	69.17	68.38	67.64	66.92	66.24	65.60	64.98
9.80	68.96	68.12	67.32	66.56	65.83	65.14	64.48	63.85
10.00	67.95	67.09	66.28	65.50	64.77	64.06	63.39	62.75

and 8. The tax consequences of premium bonds are also discussed in Chapter 6. Bonds sold originally at a discount, which are not subject to capital gains tax, are discussed in the same chapter.

Types of Municipal Bonds

The development of different types of municipal bonds since the beginnings of the 1970s has been unprecedented. More for the sake of convenience than for complete accuracy, municipal bonds are generally broken down into two categories: general obligation bonds and revenue bonds. The security for the general obligation bond is the taxing power of the state or local government. Most municipal governments depend largely on ad valorem property taxes for their revenues. State governments, on the other hand, usually do not levy real estate taxes, relying mostly on sales and income taxes, among others. The full faith and credit backing of a general obligation bond implies that all sources of revenues will be used to pay off securities, unless specifically limited. Because the taxing authority of state and local governments is considerable, the security of these bonds is generally ranked very high.

Revenue bonds are those that are issued to finance a specific revenue-generating project, and they are usually secured solely by the revenues from that project. In 1980, revenue bonds accounted for 71 percent of all new long-term municipal issues. Occasionally, revenue bonds are backed by an additional source of revenue or even the municipality's full taxing power. These hybrid obligations are called double-barreled bonds.

General Obligation Bonds

UNLIMITED TAX BONDS

These are general obligation securities that are backed by the full faith and credit of the state or local government. The taxing power of the issuer is not specifically limited.

LIMITED TAX BONDS

In some cases, state and local government taxing authority is restricted by the state constitution or by statutes. The rate of tax on assessed property value, for example, may have a ceiling. Bonds backed by such restricted taxing authority are called limited tax bonds.

FIGURE 1-4. Long Term New Issue Volume by Type of Security

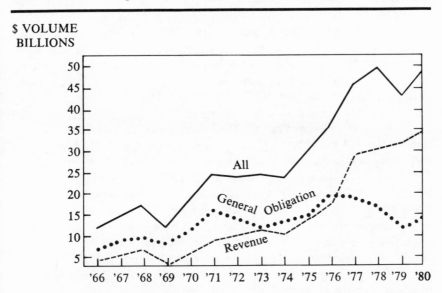

$ VOLUME
BILLIONS

SOURCE: Public Securities Association Municipal Securities Data Base

Revenue bonds have enabled municipalities to expand their use of debt financing and, in recent years, have accounted for the larger portion of the total volume of long-term securities issued.

Hybrids

SPECIAL TAX BONDS

These bonds have characteristics of both revenue and general obligation bonds. Such bonds, usually used to finance a particular project, are backed by the proceeds from one special tax—for example, a highway bond issue that is to be paid out of gasoline taxes.

MORAL OBLIGATION BONDS

Among the more controversial types of tax-exempt securities are moral obligation bonds. The moral obligation backing was first used in 1960 to support the New York State Housing Finance Agency. The Agency's bonds did not have voter approval and so were not backed by the State's full faith and credit. Instead the enabling act directed that the debt service reserve fund be replenished by the State if drawn upon, but this was not a legally enforceable obligation of the State. The reserve fund was usually. established out of bond proceeds, but at times from revenues, in an amount equal to one year's debt service. After the success of the New York State Housing Finance Agency financing, moral obligation debt flourished.

In early 1975 New York's Urban Development Corporation temporarily defaulted on $100 million of short-term notes. UDC bonds were backed by a reserve replenishment clause, or moral obligation, but its notes were not. Many thought the State should have voluntarily extended the moral obligation to the notes, and the State's refusal to pay the notes when due was a psychological blow to investor acceptance of the moral obligation backing and to the state's own general obligation debt. Even though the notes were paid three months later, the market for moral obligation issues was weakened. However, there is no instance on record of any state failing to comply with the reserve replenishment provision of moral obligation bonds when it was called for.

Short-Term Notes

The use of short-term debt by state and local governments grew astronomically beginning in the 1960s. Generally under one year in maturity, but not always, new issues of notes now regularly exceed $20 billion a year. In 1960, only $4 billion of notes were issued, and New York City was a major issuer of notes. When the City defaulted on a note issue in 1975, the use of short-term debt dropped sharply. But since then, note volume has ranged from a low of $20 billion in 1976 to a high of $27.7 billion in 1980.

Short-term borrowing serves many purposes. State and local governments use short-term financing to bridge the gap in anticipation of incoming tax revenues or new issues of bonds. Interest on notes is usually paid when they mature. Some municipalities, however, issue notes at a discount, much like Treasury bills. The following types of notes are frequently issued by state and local governments.

Tax anticipation notes—TAN's are issued in anticipation of tax receipts, and paid out of those receipts.

Revenue anticipation notes—RAN's are issued in anticipation of other sources of future revenue. Typically, the revenues are either Federal or state aid.

Bond anticipation notes—BAN's are considered the least secure of the municipality's notes. They provide a means of interim financing in anticipation of a future bond offering. Therefore, they are only as secure as the local government's ability to issue those bonds.

General obligation notes—Some state and local governments will issue notes for a variety of purposes with the full backing of the issuer. General obligation notes are the equivalent in credit quality of general obligation bonds. They are often used for the same purposes as TAN's and BAN's.

Project notes—These are the highly secure issues of the U.S. Housing and Urban Development Department. They are issued to help fund local housing and urban renewal projects and are backed both by the revenues from those projects and the full faith and credit of the U.S. government.

Revenue Bonds

Revenue bonds have enabled state and local governments to finance a wide range of projects. Bridges, airports, water and sewer treatment facilities, health care facilities, and state and local housing projects are generally financed by revenue bonds. In addition, some private corporate projects such as pollution control facilities may be financed by tax-exempt revenue bonds if they meet specific criteria under Federal law. Revenue bonds do not burden the credit capacity of the municipality itself, nor do they typically require a referendum, as do many general obligation securities. A revenue bond is in effect paid by the users of the project being financed.

Revenue bonds are issued by the state or local government, or by an authority, commission, special district, or other unit created for the purpose of issuing the bonds and constructing and operating the project. One common way to classify the variety of revenue bonds is according to the method by which funds are generated to pay the bonds off. Some examples follow.

User fees—Water, sewer, and electric revenue bonds are among the most commonly issued. The fees charged the users of these services are the sources of payment for the debt, and can be varied to meet debt obligations.

Tolls, concessions, and fees—Highway, bridge, airport, dock, and similar projects that are financed by revenue bonds raise funds through tolls, concessions, and direct fees. Restaurants along a highway, for example, pay a concession. Airlines pay fees for use of space at airports.

Lease-back—The state or local government creates a nonprofit authority or other governmental unit to issue revenue bonds and build a facility such as a school. The local government using the facility will then lease the project from the authority. It pays for those leases out of tax revenues. The lease payments are used by the issuer to pay interest on and principal of the bonds.

Industrial development bonds—These are issued directly by the municipality, a nonprofit authority, or other governmental unit in order to build a facility for a private corporation. The plant is leased to the private corporation at a rate that is sufficient to pay off the bonds. The advantage to the corporation is that the lease payments are low because the funds were raised at tax-exempt rates. Such issues are generally limited in size to $10 million by Federal legislation. Specific exceptions to the size limitation include bonds issued to finance pollution control facilities, housing, sports stadiums, industrial parks, and educational facilities.

USES OF REVENUE BONDS

A tax-exempt bond can be issued as long as it fulfills a "public purpose" as determined by state law. Many states have amended constitutions and enacted statutes that enable issuers to use tax-exempt financing for many new purposes. A description of the most popular uses of revenue bonds follows. A more detailed discussion of some of these types of bonds can be found in Chapter 7.

HOUSING REVENUE BONDS

There are several main types of housing revenue bonds. They are issued by state or local housing finance agencies or a unit of the local government, generally to support multifamily or single-family housing for low- or moderate-income families. They are also used to aid in regional redevelopment, and in some states to support housing for the aged and veterans.

State housing agencies are the primary issuers of multifamily bonds, but single-family housing issues became increasingly popular in the latter half of the 1970s. While state agencies also issue single-family bonds, units of local governments have also become frequent issuers of these securities.

There are several different structures for housing revenue bonds. In direct loan programs, the bond proceeds are used to make loans directly to a developer or several developers. For single-family issues, mortgages are typically issued directly to the home buyers out of the bond proceeds. The mortgage program is often administered by local lending institutions. Alternatively, bond proceeds are occasionally loaned directly to lending institutions, which, in turn, make mortgage loans to home buyers. These are called loan-to-lender programs.

PUBLIC UTILITY BONDS

A long-standing use of revenue bonds is to finance electric power, gas, water, and sewer systems. There are several kinds of public electric utility systems, ranging from the self-generation system with its own plant and distribution system to systems that strictly distribute electricity that is purchased from a wholesaler. There are variations of these systems as well. A public utility may supply only part of its electricity needs, or it may produce enough power to sell to other systems. The fuel source also varies, ranging from traditional coal to hydroelectric and nuclear power. By and large, however, these revenue bonds are supported by user fees, and the economic health and potential growth of the service area are key variables in determining the credit risk of the issues. This also holds true for most water, sewer, and gas issues, because the operations are usually monopolies in the area they serve.

In recent years, huge regional power supply systems have been developed that absorb enormous amounts of capital. These systems are among the largest borrowers in the tax-exempt markets. Joint action financing has also become popular in recent years. These offerings involve two or more communities that combine to finance the purchase of generating facilities or to build their own power plants.

POLLUTION CONTROL REVENUE BONDS

Pollution control bonds are the largest single category of industrial development bonds now being issued. In 1968, before passage of the Revenue and Expenditure Control Act, industrial development bonds made up some 10 percent of the long-term municipal bond market. Pollution control bonds were exempted from the restrictions the legislation placed on industrial development bonds. The financing works like most industrial development bonds. A local entity issues the bonds and leases the pollution control facilities to the corporation. The credit of the corporation is the key factor in analyzing the credit risk of the security.

HOSPITAL AND HEALTH CARE REVENUE BONDS

State legislatures have authorized units of local governments and occasionally nonprofit corporations to issue bonds to build new hospitals or make capital improvements on old ones. The debt typically has a first claim on hospital revenues. The hospitals therefore benefit from the lower costs on the tax-exempt bonds compared to alternative forms of financing.

Other Features of Municipal Bonds

There are several important features and practices that distinguish municipal securities from other kinds of securities. While less basic than those already covered, these characteristics are necessary to any grounding in the fundamentals of municipal securities. They will come up time and again as the book progresses, and a summary of the most important of these follows.

SERIAL BONDS

Unlike most other types of fixed-income securities, municipal bonds are generally issued in serial maturities. A typical offering is made up of as many as 20 or more different maturities—the serial bonds. This helps the issuer spread out debt service and stay within budget requirements. A certain number of bonds will usually come due in each year from, say, one to twenty-five years out. Generally, the longer the maturity, the higher will be the interest rate offered. A representative maturity schedule for a $100 million issue of bonds for the Municipal Electric Authority of Georgia is illustrated in Figure 1-5.

FIGURE 1-5.   Maturity Schedule

$20,395,000 Serial Bonds

Year	Amount	Coupon	Price
1981	$ 90,000	5½ %	100%
1982	150,000	5½	100
1983	160,000	5½	100
1984	170,000	5½	100
1985	180,000	5.60	100
1986	345,000	5.70	100
1987	365,000	5¾	100
1988	385,000	5.80	100
1989	1,360,000	5.90	100
1990	1,455,000	6	100
1991	1,540,000	6.10	100
1992	1,670,000	6.20	100
1993	1,775,000	6.30	100
1994	1,885,000	6.40	100
1995	2,010,000	6½	100
1996	2,140,000	6.60	100
1997	2,280,000	6.70	100
1998	2,435,000	6.70	100

$14,890,000 6⅞ % Bonds Due January 1, 2003—Price 100%
$64,715,000   7% Bonds Due January 1, 2015—Price 99%
(plus accrued interest)

SOURCE: Official statement, Municipal Electric Authority of Georgia

Serial maturities are often used to spread out debt service and help the issuer stay within budget requirements. Term bonds come due at one maturity.

In this example, there are $20,395,000 of serial bonds. There are also $79,605,000 of term bonds included in the issue. Term bonds come due at only one maturity and have become increasingly popular. They usually have a sinking fund requirement to provide for their retirement. Except for the tax exemption, term bonds are much like traditional corporate debt. Like corporate bonds, they are usually quoted by price rather than yield, and are therefore called dollar bonds.

But the large majority of municipal bonds are issued in serial maturities. The practice became widespread beginning in the 1920s. As a result, the number of municipal issues, as noted above, far exceeds the number of corporate issues. There are probably somewhere between

1.25 million and 1.75 million separate municipal issues outstanding, compared to well under 100,000 corporate issues.

BEARER BONDS VS. REGISTERED BONDS

As a matter of traditional practice most municipal securities are bearer bonds. This means that the bonds are negotiable by anyone who holds them and can prove he or she owns them. The bond certificates are simply transferred to the new owner. Attached to bearer bonds are coupons representing interest due, which the bondholder must clip and typically deposit in a bank for collection from the issuer's paying agent. On the other hand, bondholders also often have the option to register their bonds, either as to principal and interest or only as to principal. By registering the bonds with the issuer, the investor is protected from possible losses. If the bondholder is fully registered as to principal and interest, he or she will automatically receive the payments without having to clip coupons. Corporate fixed-income securities are usually registered. But registered bonds can only be transferred to someone else with the proper endorsement.

COLLECTING THE INTEREST

As stated, interest on municipal bonds is generally paid semiannually, usually on the first or fifteenth of the designated month. The last interest payment is made on the day the principal is due. Holders of bearer bonds must clip each coupon, which is numbered and dated, and present it to the issuer (usually a bank that serves as the agent) in order to receive the interest. Holders of registered bonds, as noted, will receive their interest payments automatically.

Several local governments have developed a new method of collecting coupons. They have reduced the bonds to the size of conventional checks and coded the coupons so that banks can process them by computer just as they do with checks.

The bondholder is entitled to interest beginning with a specified date on the bonds, although the bonds are often actually sold or delivered at some other date. The original date is known as the "dated date." A so-called short coupon results when the time between the dated date and the first coupon date is less than six months. A long coupon results when the first coupon date is more than six months away from the dated date.

TRADING PLUS ACCRUED INTEREST

Because most trading of municipal bonds takes place between coupon payments, it is necessary to allocate interest between buyers and sellers. The investor who sells bonds is entitled to the interest due since the last interest payment date. The convention in the municipal business is that the buyer of the bonds must pay the seller any interest due when he or she buys the bonds. If the settlement date for an investor's bond sale is March 1, for example, and the last coupon date was January 1, he or she is entitled to two months' interest from the buyer. Municipal bonds, then, trade "plus accrued interest." That is, the interest due is added on to the price of the bonds. The buyer, in turn, will collect and keep the full six months of interest due on the next coupon date.

OFFICIAL STATEMENT

New issues of corporate bonds are regulated under the securities laws by the SEC, and issuers are required to file a prospectus with the SEC that discloses all "material" information about the offering and the corporation. The SEC reviews the prospectus prior to issuance. The municipal issuer's equivalent of the prospectus is the official statement, although there is no Federal requirement that one be prepared and it is not reviewed by any Federal agency. Underwriters are required to send official statements or more abbreviated offering circulars, if they are available, to all investors according to MSRB Rule G-32.

LEGAL OPINION

One of the most important characteristics unique to municipal bonds is the bond counsel opinion. In order to be marketable, municipal bonds must carry a legal opinion. The issuer normally pays for bond counsel's services. The opinion attests to two points: first, that the bonds are legal and binding obligations of the state or local government according to the statutes, constitution, and other governing procedures of the locality; second, that the bond interest is indeed tax-exempt according to Federal and local laws.

The procedure grew out of widespread defaults of municipal bonds in the 1870s and 1880s, bonds that were issued mostly to finance railroad construction. The legality of these securities was questioned at the time. Until the 1960s and 1970s, the legal opinion had become quite routine. But new types of bond issues, the financial difficulties some municipalities have experienced, and increased Federal scrutiny, have forced bond counsel to broaden their traditional role. (See Chapter 2.)

SPECIAL CHARACTERISTICS OF THE MUNICIPAL MARKET

There are several important ways in which the municipal secondary market, or after-market, is distinct from the corporate equity or bond secondary markets. One important distinguishing characteristic of the municipal market is that all trading is done over-the-counter. There are no organized exchanges for municipal securities as there are for corporate securities.

Almost all trades in municipal securities are made on a so-called dealer basis. That is, the dealers who trade municipal securities for investors own the securities they sell to the investor or keep for their own inventory, if only temporarily, bonds bought from an investor. Their profit is the difference between the price they can sell the securities for and the price at which they bought them. This traditional business markup is known as the spread.

Also, the municipal secondary market is significantly different from other markets because of the sheer number and variety of issues. While, overall, a great deal of trading is done, trading in an individual municipal issue may be infrequent. Although no precise data are available, the volume of trading in the municipal secondary markets has been estimated by many in the industry to be one to two times as large as the new issue market in any given year. The "Blue List," a service of Standard & Poor's Corporation, lists every day those issues that dealers are publicly offering for sale. While not an indication of the trading that actually takes place, the "Blue List" typically lists some $1 billion of bonds at par value available for sale each day. Observers estimate that the "Blue List" accounts for only 30 percent to 40 percent of municipal securities available in the national market.

CALL PROVISIONS

Call provisions have become a basic feature of most sizable tax-exempt issues. They give the issuer the option to retire all or a portion of the bonds before they mature at a set price, usually at a premium to par. The provisions are generally described in the bond resolution and official statement. The call privilege, as it is sometimes referred to, is a benefit to the issuer. It gives the issuer the flexibility to refund an old issue and reduce debt costs. It can be particularly useful when interest rates have fallen since the original offering. The issuer can refund the older, high-interest issue and offer a new issue at lower rates.

Call provisions vary widely. A typical provision allows the issuer to retire bonds in ten years from the date of issue at a premium above par. Often, there are a series of call dates at descending prices. Bonds would be callable in ten years at 103, for example. In the eleventh year, they would be callable at a lower price, and so on. The earliest possible call is known as the first call.

While the call provision benefits the issuer, it can penalize the investor. The potential for capital gains is limited, and, if the bonds are called, the investor is usually left with the principal to be invested at a lower interest rate. A yield to call, therefore, is commonly computed for callable bonds especially those selling at a premium. It is simply the yield to maturity calculated to the call price and first call date. The calculation is described in the Appendix. When buying and selling these bonds, dealers will customarily tell investors both the yield to call and the yield to maturity. The Municipal Securities Rulemaking Board has adopted a rule effectively requiring that the lower of yield to call or yield to maturity be given (in terms of price) in written confirmations of transactions to investors and other dealers.

SINKING FUNDS

Sinking funds are reserves set aside yearly by the issuer to redeem term bonds over the life of the issue. Just as serial maturities help issuers spread their financial charges evenly, so too do sinking funds help level payments on the term bonds. Instead of paying off the entire issue at maturity, the issuer pays a set amount annually into the sinking fund from which bonds are redeemed on a set schedule. Sinking funds therefore add a measure of security to the bonds. The sinking fund is usually run by a trustee.

Sinking fund retirements can be optional or mandatory. A provision might require or give the option to the issuer to redeem a certain portion of the bonds beginning in ten years, or buy the bonds in the open market. If redeemed, the price is always at par or higher. Sometimes the bonds can be bought below par in the open market. If interest rates have risen over the period, pushing prices below par, the possibility of retirement will usually keep the price of the bonds up somewhat. If falling interest rates have pushed prices above par, the sinking fund provision could keep a lid on prices. The bonds to be retired are usually chosen at random by lot. The procedure should be spelled out clearly in the official statement. (See Chapter 3 for further discussion.)

CUSIP

In the mid-1960s a committee of the American Bankers Association was formed to develop a uniform method of identifying all corporate, U.S. government, and municipal securities. It was called the Committee on Uniform Security Identification Procedures, or CUSIP. The goal was to assign each security its own identification number and keep all these numbers on file.

Standard & Poor's Corporation was chosen to administer the service. The firm assigns CUSIP numbers to most municipal issues. Standard & Poor's provides a two-volume master directory of all its CUSIP listings to subscribers. Currently, there are some 1.2 million municipal issues listed in the directory.

2

The Municipal
Bond Industry

Like most industries, the municipal bond industry is made up of
many participants, each with a specific role. A distinct part is played
in the market by brokers, bankers, salesmen, traders, underwriters,
analysts, lawyers, financial advisors, accountants, state and local government treasurers and directors of finance, Federal regulators, and institutional and individual investors. But all are engaged to one end: to raise
money and to support a secondary market for debt securities of state and
local government units. And their roles can be best understood by
tracing just how each participant contributes to that process.

In 1980, $76 billion was raised for state and local governments,
compared to a little over $3.7 billion in 1950. Long-term debt issues alone
in 1980 came to $48.4 billion. The total of long-term debt and equity
raised by corporations in 1980 reached $69.4 billion. (See Figure 2-1.)

The size, diversity and local characteristics of the municipal securities
market provide opportunities for both large and small dealers and
specialists in many areas. All underwriting is done through securities
dealers or commercial bank dealers. Figure 2-2 provides a simplified
diagram of how funds flow through the new issue market. The issuer's
debt is sold by the underwriters to institutional and individual investors.
The issuer, usually through a bank acting as the paying agent, will
pay interest directly to investors, and will pay back the principal
when it is due. (See Figure 2-2.)

FIGURE 2-1   New Issues of Municipal and Corporate Capital Securities

Selected Years 1950 to 1980, by Type of Instrument

Dollar Volume (in Billions)

	Municipal Bonds			Corporate Capital Securities			
				Bonds			
	General Obligation	Revenue	Total	Public	Private Placement	Equities	Total
1950	$ 3.1	$ .6	$ 3.7	$ 2.4	$ 2.6	$ 1.5	$ 6.5
1960	5.0	2.2	7.2	4.8	3.3	2.1	10.2
1970	11.9	6.2	18.1	25.4	4.8	8.3	38.5
1975	16.0	14.7	30.7	31.5	10.2	10.9	52.6
1980	14.1	34.3	48.4	41.6	14.5	13.3	69.4

SOURCE: The Public Securities Association Data Base; The Daily Bond Buyer; Securities and Exchange Commission, *Statistical Bulletin*

The volume of capital raised in the municipal bond market has increased dramatically since 1950.

The secondary market is basically an adjunct of the new issue market. The secondary market is a term that describes all trading that goes on in securities after they have been first sold as new issues. Investors are more apt to buy a security if they know that they can resell that security at a fair market price prior to maturity. Most underwriters of municipal securities have trading departments that make secondary markets in outstanding bond issues.

The Issuers

The starting point for any municipal security, of course, is the issuer. Municipal securities are issued by state and local governmental units. Guam, Puerto Rico, the Virgin Islands, and Washington, D.C., can also issue tax-exempt bonds. The interest on bonds issued by these entities is exempt from income taxes of all state and local governments.

Most municipalities must be authorized by the state government to issue municipal securities. Authority is granted either in the state constitution or by statute. Many of these statutes also establish restrictions

**FIGURE 2-2.   The New Issue Market for Municipal Securities:
Flow of Funds**

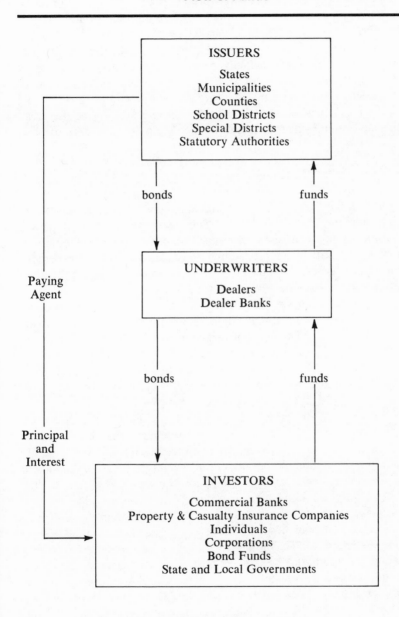

on the size and financial structure of debt. Each new issue, in turn, must usually be approved by the governing body of the municipality. Such approval may require an ordinance or resolution. In the case of general obligation bonds, approval by voter referendum is often required.

With the advent of many kinds of revenue bonds, state and local governments have established many new governmental units to issue bonds. Transportation authorities were among the first of this breed of municipal issuer. State housing authorities are now among the most common of these new entities. Nonprofit corporations have also been established to administer projects and finance them with tax-exempt debt.

THE ROLE OF BOND COUNSEL

As noted in Chapter 1, almost every municipal issue is accompanied by a legal opinion. The bond counsel addresses two main legal points. The requirements of local laws, the state constitution, judicial opinions, and enabling legislation or procedures must all be met in order for the municipal issue to be legal. The bond counsel must also be certain that the interest is exempt according to Federal laws and regulations, chiefly the applicable provisions of Section 103 of the Internal Revenue Code. An important issue, for example, is whether a particular revenue bond might be construed as an industrial revenue bond according to the Revenue and Expenditure Control Act of 1968, and therefore subject to size limitations. The Treasury arbitrage regulations apply to all types of municipal bond issues and are, therefore, closely scrutinized by bond counsel. (See Figure 2-3.)

For every issue, the bond counsel will gather all the necessary documents that assure the legality of the issue into what is termed by attorneys as a transcript of proceedings. These documents are basically those required by a bondholder to enforce rights under the bond and supporting security agreements. The transcript is passed on to the underwriter before the bond issue is delivered to investors. The counsel will also make sure the bonds are actually issued properly, and will usually examine one final bond to check signatures and terms.

In the 1960s and 1970s, the bond counsel's role broadened considerably beyond its traditional boundaries, for two main reasons. First, the variety and complexity of municipal issues, especially revenue bonds, demand considerably more legal examination. Often, bond counsel will be closely involved in drafting legislation or state constitutional amendments to enable certain kinds of revenue bonds to be issued.

FIGURE 2-3.   Sample Bond Counsel Opinion

Dear Sirs:

We have examined the transcript of proceedings relating to the issuance of $5,000,000 Highway Improvement Bonds (Seventh Series) (the "Bonds") of the City of Akron (the "City"), in the County of Summit and State of Ohio, being a series of bonds numbered from 182112 to 183111, inclusive, dated .... bearing interest at the rate of ....% per annum, payable December 1, 1979 and semiannually thereafter, maturing serially on December 1 from 1980 to 2004, inclusive, and issued for the purpose of paying costs of improving designated expressways and streets in the manner described in the ordinance authorizing the Bonds.

We have also examined the law under authority of which the Bonds are issued and executed Bond No. 182112, and from this examination we are of the opinion that the Bonds constitute valid and legal general obligations of the City and that the principal of and interest on the Bonds, unless paid from other sources and subject to the provisions of the federal Bankruptcy law and other laws affecting creditors' rights, are to be paid from the proceeds of the levy of ad valorem taxes on all property in the City subject to ad valorem taxes levied by the City, which taxes are unlimited as to amount or rate.

We are further of the opinion that, under the law existing on the date of this opinion, the interest on the bonds is exempt from federal income tax, Ohio corporate franchise tax, Ohio personal income tax and municipal income taxes in Ohio.

Respectfully submitted,

SOURCE: Squire, Sanders & Dempsey

The legal opinion is virtually a requirement for any significant municipal offering. Counsel must attest that the bonds have been issued legally, according to state and local law and that the interest is exempt from income tax according to Federal law.

Second, abuses in the early 1970s, coupled with the municipal financial problems in the latter half of the 1970s, have put issuers, underwriters, and bond counsel on guard against their own liability in such cases. Many bond counsels have expanded their examination practices as a result. Some counsel do their own financial analyses of state and local governments. (See Chapter 9 for a fuller discussion of the potential liability of counsel.)

A half-dozen large law firms do a great deal of the bond counsel work on a national basis. Another dozen or so large firms are solidly established in various regions of the country. But like many other groups in the municipal bond industry, some hundreds of local law firms do much if not most of the bond counsel work in their own smaller communities.

FINANCIAL ADVISORS

State and local governments generally are not equipped to develop and market a bond issue on their own. Financial advisors are employed to analyze the credit needs of the community, construct an issue, help choose an underwriter, or organize a competitive sale, deal with the rating agencies, and advise on other matters of importance. The scope of their work will overlap that of the underwriters. A financial advisor can act as the underwriter for the issue, although the practice is becoming increasingly rare for large issues. The Municipal Securities Rulemaking Board has adopted a rule to cover possible conflicts between advisors and underwriters (see Chapter 4). Financial advisors are generally paid on a fee basis for their services.

Aside from financial advice, projects in communities often require the advice of other kinds of specialists. There are firms, for example, that consult solely on the financial, engineering, and architectural aspects of airports. Similarly, there are specialists in transportation facilities and public utilities. The opinions of such consultants are often important in attracting voter approval for projects and investor acceptance of bonds that are backed by the revenues of such projects.

The Investors

Three classes of investors dominate the municipal marketplace: commercial banks, fire and casualty insurance companies, and households. The principal characteristic of all buyers of municipal bonds is that they are in a sufficiently high tax bracket to benefit from the tax-exempt feature of municipal bonds. Traditionally, tax-exempt bonds are considered suitable for individual investors in the 35 percent marginal tax bracket or higher. That is, municipal rates are usually about 35 percent lower than equivalent corporate rates.

Commercial banks today are the major buyers of municipal securities. The banks buy them for their own account as an asset in their banking portfolio. Twenty years ago, the commercial banks owned 28 percent of all municipal issues outstanding, but since then have increased their share of ownership. In 1980, they owned about 46 percent of all outstanding issues. The reason for the growing appetite for municipals was the more aggressive investing strategy that the country's largest banks adopted in the 1960s. Also, bank assets grew faster than the economy over the period, and for the most part profits stayed high. The banks found the tax-exempt municipal issues attractive.

The municipal buying activity of fire and casualty insurance companies has also increased. Their share of the market jumped from around 17 percent in 1973 to about 25 percent in 1980. The profitability of these firms grew over this period and the tax-exempt bonds, especially the longer-term issues, proved attractive.

Both commercial banks and casualty insurance companies are cyclical buyers of municipal bonds because their profits can swing widely up and down. When they are less profitable, they buy far fewer tax-exempt bonds. Because these institutions account for about two-thirds of the ownership of municipal securities, the cyclicality of their profits can affect municipal interest rates.

Households are the remaining large buyers of municipal bonds. Households include individual investors, trusts run by banks and trust companies, and bond funds. Overall, the proportion of municipal securities owned by households has declined significantly in the past two decades. In 1960, households owned more than 43 percent of outstanding issues, and in 1980 the level fell to 19 percent.

The Dealers

To the dealer departments of commercial banks and securities firms belongs the enormous task of underwriting, marketing, and trading municipal securities. Most major stock brokerage firms have municipal bond departments that underwrite and trade state and local government securities. Similarly, many major commercial banks have such departments. There is another class of dealer that operates solely in the municipal market. Some of these firms specialize only in underwriting and financial advisory, sometimes in a particular type of security such as housing bonds. Others do mostly "retail" business—that is, trade with investors, often individual investors. Still other firms trade only for dealers. These are the municipal bond brokers, or "brokers' brokers." In 1979, there were some 1,350 dealers and 350 bank dealers registered with the SEC to do business in municipal securities, although only about one-third were actively involved in the market.

General obligation bonds are, with some exceptions, the only type of municipal security that commercial banks can underwrite. The Glass-Steagall Act of 1933 prohibited commercial banks from participating in the underwriting and trading of municipal revenue bond issues as well as corporate securities. However, rulings of Federal bank regulatory authorities have allowed commercial banks to underwrite certain types of revenue bond issues, such as housing' and education revenue bonds. In 1979, these types of revenue bonds represented about 40 percent of all revenue bonds issued.

COMPETITIVE vs. NEGOTIATED UNDERWRITING

Most general obligation bonds are underwritten on a competitive basis. Two or more groups of underwriters will bid for an issue, trying to come up with the lowest bid to the issuer. The issuer chooses the group that will buy the bonds for the lowest interest cost. The underwriters, in turn, will pay that price for the bonds no matter how successful they are in selling those bonds to investors afterward. Dealers and dealer banks compete alike in this market.

Revenue bonds, on the other hand, are often underwritten on a negotiated basis. The municipality or authority chooses one underwriter or group of underwriters to sell the bonds. There is no competitive bidding. The underwriters try to produce the lowest interest rates on the issue that the market will bear, but they also perform many other services for the issuer.

To facilitate the underwriting of all but the smallest issues, several dealers will form selling groups called syndicates. The leader or leaders of the syndicate are called managers or co-managers. They will do the largest share of the underwriting and selling. One or two senior or lead managers will do the administrative and organizational work, for which the client pays a management fee and the manager takes the largest portion of the management fee.

Dealers often make markets in securities they have underwritten after the sales take place. Many dealers, of course, also trade actively in other municipal securities, and secondary market trading is one of the key activities for most major dealers.

A typical municipal department is divided into six distinct functions. A brief description of the activities of each follows. (See Figure 2-4.)

FIGURE 2-4. **Typical Municipal Securities Department**

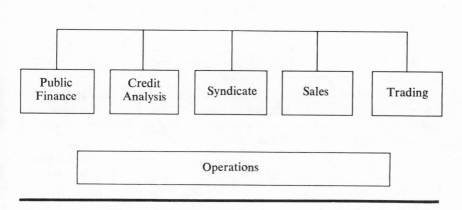

UNDERWRITING (Syndicate)

A department will have one or more individuals whose full-time responsibility is to work on competitive and negotiated underwritings. They will be primarily responsible for setting prices and yields on the new issues their firm underwrites each week. That requires attending price meetings, a tradition largely limited to a handful of major cities, or working over the phone with dealers in other regions of the country. Several of the large Chicago and West Coast bank dealers maintain underwriting and trading offices in New York that have responsibility for making decisions to commit the banks' funds. Underwriters work closely with traders and salesmen to determine the marketability and appropriate yields for an issue.

TRADING

Traders maintain the secondary market for securities by actively buying bonds and selling bonds to other dealers and investors in the secondary market. This requires a large inventory of bonds to service clients, because there are so many kinds of issues. An effective trader should be familiar at all times with the bonds that are available for sale or purchase in the market.

Many trading departments will have several traders. Typically, one will specialize in term bonds, or dollar bonds. Another trader might specialize in notes, another in housing issues, and so on.

SALES

A dealer firm will frequently have several salesmen responsible for making direct contact with investors. They often sit at the trading desk with the underwriters and traders and attempt to arrange sales of securities during the underwriting of a new issue. Salesmen's responsibilities are broken down in several ways. A common method is to divide the territory geographically. Another method is to divide the salesmen according to clients they have developed over the years.

Securities firms with many individual investors will often have a sales liaison force sitting near the trading desk that works with the account executives in branch offices. The branch offices will contact the sales liaison staff at the trading desk when there is an order. The liaison staff passes the order to the traders. Several large securities firms have regional trading areas that duplicate their main office trading operation on a smaller scale. A sales force and liaison staff in these regional offices work in much the same way as they would in the main office.

The traders, underwriters, and salesmen generally sit in a large trading room within proximity to each other and before telephone consoles that connect them with clients, other dealers, and their branch offices. In addition, most larger trading operations have one person assigned to do computations for underwriting bids. Some firms have their own computer models, but most subscribe to outside time-sharing services to calculate bids.

PUBLIC FINANCE

This is the group that seeks new negotiated underwriting business for the dealer firm. This same group will also usually do financial advisory work for a fee. Commercial banks, which do not participate to a great extent in negotiated underwritings because of the restrictions of the Glass-Steagall Act, will often have a financial advisory group as part of their municipal bond department. However, some commercial banks do have active new business departments to concentrate in housing and education revenue bonds.

MUNICIPAL RESEARCH

The increased awareness in recent years of the potential for municipal governments to experience financial difficulties has led dealers to place greater emphasis on research into the credit worthiness of municipal issuers. At one time, the rating agencies were far and away the prominent sources of credit information on municipal bonds. These days, dealers as well as investors are expanding their own efforts. Research staffs at bank dealers, securities firms, and insurance companies have grown by multiples of two and three. The research department in an underwriting firm will usually prepare a short opinion on important competitive or negotiated issues coming to market that the firm might bid on. This helps the underwriters and traders set yields on the issues.

Similar to equity research, municipal research is also provided directly to institutional and individual clients by many dealer firms. The general principles of municipal research are discussed in Chapter 7.

OPERATIONS

This function has become more complex and important in recent years. Operations involve the processing of securities and payments, as well as the accounting for the municipal department—essentially, the traditional back office activities. The adoption by the MSRB of industry-wide requirements for orders, record keeping, and confirmations has significantly expanded the functions of the operations group. The operations rules of the MSRB are discussed in greater detail in Chapters 4, 5, and 9. Among other duties, the operations group processes orders and payments, checks and delivers securities, issues confirmations, and maintains customer accounts and other required documentation.

Bond Brokers

The bond brokers or brokers' brokers play a very important part in the workings of the municipal market. Municipal bond brokers trade only for municipal bond dealers and dealer banks—that is, they do not work directly with investors, institutional or individual. Essentially, dealers will use brokers to facilitate a trade if they cannot make it more efficiently themselves. Dealers, for example, will often try to sell bonds in inventory through brokers. They can ask a broker to seek bids on the bonds from other dealers. This is known as the "bid-wanted" business. On the other hand, a dealer may be looking for particular bonds for a customer and tell the bond broker that he would be willing to buy them at a specified yield or price. In this instance, the broker will seek these bonds from other dealers. There are about two dozen active municipal bond brokers in the country, mostly located in New York City.

The Rating Agencies

Because of the large number of different issues in the marketplace, bond ratings often play a greater role in the municipal securities market than in the corporate markets. A rating is considered obligatory for the sale of any major issue. It ranks each security according to what the rating agencies believe is its credit worthiness.

The two dominant agencies in the ratings field are Moody's Investors Service, Inc. and Standard & Poor's Corporation. Fitch Investors Services Inc. also rates bonds. All three are located in New York City. Moody's has been rating municipal bonds longer than Standard & Poor's, having started in 1918. It now has some 15,000 municipal bonds rated and rates another 4,500 new issues a year. Moody's also rates short-term notes. Standard & Poor's started rating municipal bonds in 1940 and has about 7,000 ratings outstanding. It rates another 1,500 new issues each year. Standard & Poor's will not rate most types of short-term notes, or certain kinds of revenue bonds.

The rating agencies charge fees for their bond ratings based on the size of the issue and the amount of analysis needed. The ratings Moody's and Standard & Poor's assign differ on about 20 percent of those issues rated by both agencies. At both firms the ratings must be approved by a ratings committee after analysis by individual analysts. Most major issuers communicate regularly with the agencies, and underwriters are often involved with making presentations on behalf of issuers to the agencies. The rating agencies review their ratings regularly and request updated information. In addition, they provide a review process for municipalities seeking to improve their ratings. The municipal securities ratings assigned by Moody's and Standard & Poor's are described in Figure 2-5.

Municipal bonds, particularly smaller issues, are also marketed on a non-rated basis. In 1980, 22.3 percent of long-term issues that came to market were not rated by Moody's.

FIGURE 2-5.   Guide to the Municipal Bond Ratings of Moody's and Standard and Poor's

---

KEY TO STANDARD & POOR'S MUNICIPAL RATINGS

AAA Bonds rated "AAA" have the highest rating assigned by Standard & Poor's to a debt obligation. Capacity to pay interest and repay principal is extremely strong.

AA Bonds rated "AA" have a very strong capacity to pay interest and repay principal and differ from the highest-rated issues only in a small degree.

A Bonds rated "A" have a strong capacity to pay interest and repay principal, although they are somewhat more susceptible to the adverse effects of changes in circumstances and economic conditions than bonds in higher-rated categories.

BBB Bonds rated "BBB" are regarded as having an adequate capacity to pay interest and repay principal. Whereas they normally exhibit adequate protection parameters, adverse economic conditions or changing circumstances are more likely to lead to a weakened capacity to pay interest and repay principal for bonds in this category than for bonds in higher-rated categories.

BB Bonds rated "BB," "B," "CCC," and "CC" are regarded, on balance,
B as predominantly speculative with respect to capacity to pay interest
CCC and repay principal in accordance with the terms of the obligation.
CC "BB" indicates the lowest degree of speculation and "CC" the highest degree of speculation. While such bonds will likely have some quality and protective characteristics, these are outweighed by large uncertainties or major risk exposures to adverse conditions.

C The rating "C" is reserved for income bonds on which no interest is being paid.

D Bonds rated "D" are in default, and payment of interest and/or repayment of principal is in arrears.

Plus (+) or Minus (−): The ratings from "AA" to "BB" may be modified by the addition of a plus or minus sign to show relative standing within the major rating categories.

Provisional Ratings: The letter "p" indicates that the rating is provisional. A provisional rating assumes the successful completion of the project being financed by the bonds being rated and indicates that payment of debt service requirements is largely or entirely dependent upon the successful and timely completion of the project. This rating, however, while addressing credit quality subsequent to completion of the project, makes no comment on the likelihood of, or the risk of default upon failure of, such completion. The investor should exercise his own judgment with respect to such likelihood and risk.

NR Indicates that no rating has been requested, that there is insufficient information on which to base a rating, or that Standard & Poor's does not rate a particular type of obligation as a matter of policy.

KEY TO MOODY'S MUNICIPAL RATINGS

Aaa

Bonds which are rated Aaa are judged to be of the best quality. They carry the smallest degree of investment risk and are generally referred to as "gilt edge." Interest payments are protected by a large or by an exceptionally stable margin and principal is secure. While the various protective elements are likely to change, such changes as can be visualized are most unlikely to impair the fundamentally strong position of such issues.

Aa

Bonds which are rated Aa are judged to be of high quality by all standards. Together with the Aaa group they comprise what are generally known as high grade bonds. They are rated lower than the best bonds because margins of protection may not be as large as in Aaa securities or fluctuation of protective elements may be of greater amplitude or there may be other elements present which make the long-term risks appear somewhat larger than in Aaa securities.

A

Bonds which are rated A possess many favorable investment attributes and are to be considered as upper medium grade obligations. Factors giving security to principal and interest are considered adequate, but elements may be present which suggest a susceptibility to impairment sometime in the future.

Baa

Bonds which are rated Baa are considered as medium grade obligations, i.e., they are neither highly protected nor poorly secured.

Interest payments and principal security appear adequate for the present but certain protective elements may be lacking or may be characteristically unreliable over any great length of time. Such bonds lack outstanding investment characteristics and in fact have speculative characteristics as well.

Ba

Bonds which are rated Ba are judged to have speculative elements; their future cannot be considered as well assured. Often the protection of interest and principal payments may be very moderate, and thereby not well safeguarded during both good and bad times over the future. Uncertainty of position characterizes bonds in this class.

B

Bonds which are rated B generally lack characteristics of the desirable investment. Assurance of interest and principal payments or of maintenance of other terms of the contract over any long period of time may be small.

Caa

Bonds which are rated Caa are of poor standing. Such issues may be in default or there may be present elements of danger with respect to principal or interest.

Ca

Bonds which are rated Ca represent obligations which are speculative in a high degree. Such issues are often in default or have other marked shortcomings.

C

Bonds which are rated C are the lowest rated class of bonds, and issues so rated can be regarded as having extremely poor prospects of ever attaining any real investment standing.

CON. (. . .)

Bonds for which the security depends upon the completion of some act or the fulfillment of some condition are rated conditionally. These are bonds secured by (a) earnings of projects under construction, (b) earnings of projects unseasoned in operating experience, (c) rentals which begin when facilities are completed, or (d) payments to which some other limiting condition attaches. Parenthetical rating denotes probable credit stature upon completion of construction or elimination of basis of condition.

Those bonds in the A and Baa groups which Moody's believes possess the strongest investment attributes are designated by the symbols A 1 and Baa 1.

Key to Moody's Short-Term Loan Ratings

MIG 1

Loans bearing this designation are of the best quality, enjoying strong protection from established cash flows of funds for their servicing or from established and broad-based access to the market for refinancing, or both.

MIG 2

Loans bearing this designation are of high quality, with margins of protection ample although not so large as in the preceding group.

MIG 3

Loans bearing this designation are of favorable quality, with all security elements accounted for but lacking the undeniable strength of the preceding grades. Market access for refinancing, in particular, is likely to be less well established.

MIG 4

Loans bearing this designation are of adequate quality, carrying specific risk but having protection commonly regarded as required of an investment security and not distinctly or predominantly speculative.

SOURCES: Moody's Investors Service and Standard and Poor's Corporation

The Qualifications Examinations

One of the first rules the MSRB adopted requires that all persons involved with "any transaction" in municipal securities must pass a qualifying examination. As with corporate securities employees, the exams are administered by the National Association of Securities Dealers (NASD).

The Board has established three distinct classes of municipal securities employees, according to Rule G-3, and has developed a different qualifying exam for each class. The great majority of employees are termed municipal securities representatives. They include anyone who underwrites, trades or sells municipal securities, does research or offers investment advice, provides financial or advisory services to issuers, or is involved in "any activities other than those specifically enumerated above which involve communication, directly or indirectly, with public investors in municipal securities." Clerical personnel are generally not included in this group.

There are two important exemptions for the qualifications test. First, anyone who was employed in these activities before December 1, 1975, does not have to take the examination. Second, anyone who has already passed the NASD examination for general securities need not take the municipal securities exam. New employees may take the general securities exam in lieu of the municipal securities exam. In addition to taking the qualifying exam, all new municipal securities representatives must serve an apprenticeship of 90 days on the job before they can transact any business. The passing score for the exam is set by the MSRB. An apprentice representative can take the exam again after 30 days, but must pass the exam before the end of a 180-day time limit or cease to perform the functions of a municipal securities professional.

The two other classes of municipal securities employees are the municipal securities principals and the financial and operations principals. The municipal securities principal is essentially in charge of—or at least has some supervisory role in—the municipals operation. Each firm must have at least one principal, and in some cases two. The financial and operations principal is the person designated to be in charge of preparing and filing financial reports to the SEC or any other regulatory agency. There is a separate exam for principals and for financial and operations principals. Principals who were performing these functions before December 1, 1975, are exempted from the exams. Those financial and operations principals who are already qualified as such under the general securities examination are also exempted.

3

The Issuers

According to U.S. Census Bureau figures, there are some 80,000 state and local governments in this country. Of these, perhaps 50,000 have issued municipal securities. In addition, there are hundreds of state and local entities, such as housing agencies and transportation authorities, established to issue bonds to finance public purpose projects.

Unlike the market for corporate debt securities, the municipal securities market consists largely of smaller issues. The Public Securities Association estimates that, on average, over the past ten years, about 44 percent of municipal bond issues each year have been for $1 million or less, and 81 percent of all issues have been $5 million or less. On the other hand, the bulk of the dollar volume of new issues, particularly in recent years, is concentrated in the larger issues. Most large issues are $100 million to $200 million but the New York Municipal Assistance Corporation has come to market for as much as $1 billion at one time.

The history of municipal debt predates that of corporate debt by some two thousand years. There are accounts of borrowing by ancient cities and even of occasional defaults. Careful records of U.S. municipal bond data were started only in 1843, although borrowing by some U.S. cities dates back to the seventeenth century. By the 1840s, many local governments were in the debt market. In 1843, there was some $25 million of debt outstanding, and growth was to explode in the next two decades. Bonds were issued to finance improvements for the rapidly developing cities, as well as the burgeoning system of free public education.

After the Civil War, much of the local debt was raised to build the railroads. These bond issues were very similar to today's industrial revenue bonds. The Panic of 1873, and the several years of depression that followed, put an abrupt, if temporary, halt to the rapid growth of municipal debt. Widespread defaults jolted the municipal bond market. New state statutes were passed that put restrictions on the issuance of local debt, and some states even wrote these restrictions into their constitutions. The legality of the railroad bonds was widely challenged, giving rise to the marketwide demand for an opinion of bond counsel to accompany each issue.

Once the economy started to move forward, municipal debt resumed its rapid growth into the beginning of the twentieth century. The Great Depression of the 1930s set the market back again, although defaults were not as severe as in the 1870s. The amount of municipal debt outstanding fell during World War II as resources were devoted to the war effort. But after the war, municipal debt burst into a new period of rapid growth for a widening array of new uses. Just after World War II, municipal debt per capita was $145. By 1979, per capita debt had risen to $1,382.

The Theory of Municipal Debt: Pay-as-You-Use vs. Pay-as-You-Acquire

Corporations borrow to build facilities or to invest otherwise to improve returns. The resulting profits are used to pay back the debt. Without the profit motive, the justification for municipal borrowing has historically centered on the purposes of borrowing and who should pay for the debt. Proponents of the liberal use of debt financing argue that new facilities should be paid for over time by the people who are benefiting—the pay-as-you-use approach. A community that pays for a new water system immediately, goes the argument, is unfairly taking on a burden that should also be borne by future taxpayers who will get continuing use out of the water system. Furthermore, a growing city will be better able to afford the debt payments over time, and new projects today may very well be necessary to aid a municipality's growth. With this in mind, policymakers often want the repayment schedule for any municipal debt raised to finance a project to coincide with the minimum expected life of the facilities.

The theory behind municipal revenue bonds is, in part, an extension of this pay-as-you-use philosophy. Revenue bonds are paid off from revenues generated by the particular project being financed. The beneficiaries of the project—the customers or users—are paying off the debt, not the community as a whole.

In a time when debt financing has become a way of life for corporations, municipalities, and consumers alike, any theoretical justification for borrowing may seem superfluous. But when the national economy has turned down in the past, the pay-as-you-use approach has come under heavy criticism. In belt-tightening periods such as the 1930s, state and local officials have favored the pay-as-you-acquire philosophy. Simply put, new projects should be paid for immediately.

It is safe to conclude that the accepted view of fiscal probity for state and local governments will swing with the health of the nation's economy. A recent example of how political attitudes affect municipal debt was the passage of Proposition 13 in 1978 as an amendment to the California state constitution. The amendment limits the property tax to 1 percent of full value rather than taking any direct action to limit debt. But the result was that the issuance of general obligation debt in the state slowed substantially.

The Uses of Municipal Debt

The everyday operating expenses of state and local governments must be paid from current tax and other revenues. Municipal debt is used generally to finance capital projects only.

The major purposes for which municipal debt has been issued over the last twenty years are shown in Figure 3-1. In the 1950s, highways, water and sewer, and electric systems were the major uses of debt. In the 1960s, college dormitories and transportation were financed heavily with tax-exempt bonds. In the 1970s, public power systems, housing, and pollution control equipment for corporations have been financed largely by municipal bonds. The popularity of the revenue bond, which puts no direct strain on a municipality's finances, has given state and local governments much more latitude than ever before in financing public purpose projects. (See Figure 3-1.)

AUTHORITIES AND SPECIAL DISTRICTS

Early in the twentieth century, state and local governments began to create new debt-issuing entities called authorities and special districts.

FIGURE 3-1. Major Uses of Municipal Debt, 1966-1980, as a Percentage of Total Long-Term Borrowing

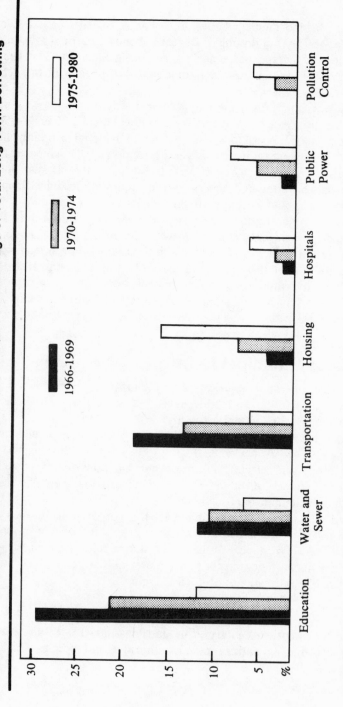

SOURCE: Public Securities Association Municipal Securities Data Base

Changes in the major uses of debt financing over the years reflect both the evolution of new financing techniques and the public's demand for government-provided services.

They were formed often to encompass a wide geographical area that crossed political boundaries, or as an ongoing entity to administer and raise money for a single kind of project. Two prominent early authorities were the Port of New York Authority and the Triborough Bridge Authority. The debt issues of such authorities are exempt from Federal taxes, and they were made marketable with the help of conservative bond covenants and ample reserve funds. Occasionally a state or local government will stand fully behind the debt of a special district or authority, or back it with a moral obligation. Often, however, the issues of these entities are straightforward revenue bonds.

Today, authorities and special districts of all types are found across the country. The majority of states, for example, have housing authorities. Special district bonds are commonly used to finance water, sewer, and utility services where user charges are involved. Authorities are typically created to finance and construct housing, roads, airports, docking facilities, sports arenas, and convention centers. The relative importance of statutory authorities as issuers of municipal securities has increased dramatically during the 1970s. (See Figures 3-2 and 3-3.)

THE FINANCING DECISIONS

This book does not offer a course on municipal fiscal management. The political, economic, and financial factors are diverse and complicated.

FIGURE 3-2. Municipal Borrowing by Type of Issuer, Selected Years, 1966-1980

As a Percentage of Total Long-Term Borrowing

	1966	1970	1974	1980
States	21.0%	22.0%	15.9%	10.4%
Counties	6.6	9.1	8.7	10.1
Municipalities	20.9	26.3	27.0	19.2
School Districts	14.2	11.8	9.2	5.1
Special Districts	6.9	6.4	5.3	2.7
Statutory Authorities	30.4	24.4	33.9	52.5
				100.0%

SOURCE: Public Securities Association Municipal Securities Data Base

The relative importance of statutory authorities as issuers of municipal securities has increased dramatically during the 1970s.

**FIGURE 3-3.   Major Uses of Special District and Statutory
Authority Bonds in 1980**

(Amounts in Thousands)

Use of Proceeds	Special District	Statutory Authority
Education: Total	40,469	1,978,599
Ports, Airports	41,100	496,896
Water and Sewer	489,413	707,703
Electric and Gas	125,000	2,711,810
Public Housing	00	11,941,683
Hospitals	29,812	2,393,047

SOURCE: Public Securities Association Municipal Securities Data Base

The debt burden a community can tolerate, the economic maturity of
and prospects for the local economy, and the legal restrictions on borrowing are key considerations that are discussed in Chapter 7 on Credit
Analysis. Legal and financial advisors are available for help, of course.

But today the municipal finance officer clearly has more flexibility
than ever before in arranging finances. The advent of revenue bonds
alone gives state and local governments a range of alternative financing
methods that neither require a voter referendum nor will add any debt
to the community's balance sheet. The frequent use of short-term debt
to bridge the gaps in longer-term financing has also increased the
municipalities' financial options. In short, borrowing has become an
important tool for the management of many state and local governmental
units. Some basic financing considerations for issuers follow.

DEBT REPAYMENT SCHEDULES

Arrangement of a great deal of serial bond schedules affords flexibility
to financial officers, lending themselves especially well to meeting annual
budget considerations. Serial maturities of issues can be constructed to
dovetail with expected revenues and outlays. Interest and principal
payments can be set up to produce a nearly level debt service year in
and year out. Balloon maturities with most principal payments near the end
of the issue can be worked out. Sinking funds provide regular repayment
on term bonds. (See Figure 3-4.)

The choice of maturities also depends on marketability. A diversity of maturities will usually broaden the appeal of an issue, attracting a variety of investors. The level of interest rates will also influence decisions concerning maturities. For example, if short-term interest rates are considered to be unusually low or demand for short-term issues is strong, an issue weighted more heavily toward shorter-maturity serial bonds can be constructed.

CALL PROVISIONS

The cost to the issuer of the call privilege is generally a higher interest rate on the issue. Investors will often demand a higher yield for a security with a call provision because the potential for capital gain is limited. Also, if the bonds are called away before maturity, the investor may be left with his or her principal to be invested at a lower interest rate. The question to the issuer is whether the advantages of the call privilege are sufficient to justify the higher interest cost. When interest rates appear to be high and volatile, a call provision is obviously most desirable. It enables the issuer to refund an issue and raise money again when rates are lower.

Thirty days before bonds are to be called, the issuer generally notifies investors through an advertisement in a financial publication. The advertisements will state which bonds are being redeemed and how the bondholder will receive payment. The call provision normally states in which order bonds will be called, usually in reverse order of maturity. Investors with unregistered bonds who have not seen or been notified of the call will typically be notified by the paying agent when a coupon is sent in for payment.

NEGOTIATED vs. COMPETITIVE SALES

The advantages of competitive bidding to the issuer is the competition on the open market. However, for lesser-known issuers, or complicated offerings, open sales may not bring many bidders. A negotiated sale may be the better alternative. Investment bankers argue that, in negotiated sales, the dealers' salesmen have more time to prepare. They will expend more effort before the sale because they know they have the issue to sell. The dealers add that they have more flexibility in timing

FIGURE 3-4. Maturity Schedule and Debt Service Schedule of a Level Debt Service Issue

$5,200,000
City of Anderson, Indiana
Electric Utility Revenue Bonds
Series A
Maturity Schedule

Principal payable annually on January 1 and interest payable semiannually on January 1 and July 1 (beginning January 1, 1981, eight months from the dated date of the Bonds) payable at the principal office of the Anderson Banking Company, in the City of Anderson, Indiana, or at the principal office of the Merchants National Bank & Trust Company, Indianapolis, Indiana. The Bonds will be in $5,000 denominations and may be registered as to the principal only. The Series A Bonds will be subject to redemption prior to maturity on and after January 1, 1990 as set forth herein.

Due	Amount	Coupon	Price
1981	$155,000	7.80%	6.25%
1982	160,000	7.80	6.30
1983	170,000	7.80	6.35
1984	180,000	7.80	6.40
1985	190,000	7.80	6.50
1986	200,000	7.80	6.60
1987	215,000	7.80	6.75
1988	230,000	7.80	6.90
1989	240,000	7.90	7.00
1990	255,000	7.90	7.15
1991	270,000	7.90	7.30
1992	290,000	7.90	7.50
1993	310,000	7.90	7.70
1994	330,000	7.90	100
1995	350,000	8.00	100
1996	375,000	8.10	100
1997	400,000	8.20	100
1998	425,000	8.25	100
1999	455,000	8.30	100

Serial maturities provide issuers with a flexible tool for meeting governmental budget requirements. In the debt service schedule illustrated below, interest and principal payments have been set up to produce a nearly level debt service each year for the life of the bonds.

Debt Service Schedule

The following table shows debt service to maturity on the Bonds. There is presently outstanding no other indebtedness incurred on behalf of the Utility.

Year Ending December 31	Principal	Interest	Total
1980	$ —	$ —	$ —
1981	155,000	478,014	633,014
1982	160,000	396,578	556,578
1983	170,000	383,708	553,708
1984	180,000	370,058	550,058
1985	190,000	355,628	545,628
1986	200,000	340,418	540,418
1987	215,000	324,233	539,233
1988	230,000	306,878	536,878
1989	240,000	288,428	528,428
1990	255,000	268,875	523,875
1991	270,000	248,138	518,138
1992	290,000	226,018	516,018
1993	310,000	202,318	512,318
1994	330,000	177,038	507,038
1995	350,000	150,003	500,003
1996	375,000	120,815	495,815
1997	400,000	89,228	489,228
1998	425,000	55,296	480,296
1999	455,000	18,883	473,883

a negotiated offering, as well as in developing a package that suits current market conditions. Novel and complicated issues can especially benefit from close work with the underwriters. The syndicate that handles a negotiated offering generally receives a larger spread than the winner of a competitive offering.

NET INTEREST COST vs. TRUE INTEREST COST

The issuer must also decide on what basis competing syndicates will calculate their bids for the bonds. The traditional method is an arithmetic calculation known as the net interest cost (NIC). There has been a movement in recent years, however, to adopt a different calculation known as the true interest cost (TIC). This increasingly accepted method of calculation takes into account the time value of money to produce a more accurate indication of the true interest cost of an issue. In spite of the argument now made by some that the NIC may cause an issuer to choose a more expensive bid, many issuers still prefer the more traditional method of calculation. As a result, bidding constraints have been devised to help assure that the costs of bids calculated with the NIC are consistent with the true interest cost of the issue. A full discussion of NIC, TIC, and these rules can be found in the Appendix.

State and Local Government Accounting

Government accounting necessarily differs in several important ways from business accounting. Business accounting is ultimately concerned with the profits of the owners. There is no such clear-cut measure of success for governments. While businesses must match sales to the expenses that were incurred in making those sales, governments must be certain that resources are sufficient to meet outlays. Businesses try to maximize profits. Governments must meet the annual budget. To the owner of a business, the consolidation of all expenses and revenues of a business, no matter how diversified, makes sense. But government revenue sources for certain services have little to do with revenues raised for other sources. Segregated accounts are usually more appropriate. Government regulations also often require that accounts be kept separately.

Such differences have resulted in a separate set of accounting principles for government developed by the National Council on Governmental Accounting. The NCGA is affiliated with the Municipal Finance Officers Association and first started setting principles in 1934. In 1968, the organization produced a standard reference, *Governmental Accounting, Auditing, and Financial Reporting*. In 1979, the principles were updated and restated in another publication, *Governmental Accounting and Financial Reporting Principles*. The Financial Accounting Standards Board, which sets business accounting standards, has also undertaken a study of governmental accounting. The two accounting organizations are working together to produce a common approach to the subject. The most important accounting principles are discussed below.

FUND ACCOUNTING

To account for the diverse activities of the governmental unit, accounts are divided into separate funds. As noted, statutes and regulations often require that resources, and the areas to which they are applied, must be accounted for separately. And government officials argue that fund accounting makes good sense anyway because it gives a clearer picture of the extent to which the various revenue sources are used to finance different categories of expenditures.

Each fund includes a set of accounts to record the revenues, expenditures (or expenses), assets, liabilities, and fund balances (or equity) of the activities of that fund. The NCGA specifies eight major types of funds that fall into three categories. A governmental unit may require one or several funds of a type or, on the other hand, may not require all eight funds. The eight types of funds are described below.

Governmental funds—Most typical government functions are financed through these funds.

The general fund—This is normally the largest of the funds. It essentially accounts for all financial resources other than those accounted for in any other fund. Most current operations of the government are recorded here. Such taxes as property taxes, income taxes, and sales taxes will be typically recorded in the general fund.

Special revenue fund—This fund records proceeds from specific sources that are usually earmarked for a special use, such as the care of parks, museums, or highways. Special assessments, major capital projects, and expendable trusts are recorded in other funds.

Capital projects fund—Any resources used for the acquisition and construction of capital facilities are accounted for here. Exceptions are those projects financed by the special assessment and enterprise funds. Formerly called the bonds fund, the capital projects fund was created because so many capital projects are no longer funded with bonds but from other sources such as direct revenues and grants. Separate capital projects funds are commonly set up for individual projects.

Debt service fund—This fund records the payment of interest and principal on long-term general obligation debt, as well as the accumulation of resources to pay off the debt.

Special assessment fund—Special assessments are often levied against property that has been specifically benefited by construction or improvement of streets, sidewalks, sewers, and so on. This fund accounts for those special assessments.

Proprietary funds—These funds account for the operations of a government that are similar to businesses. Accounting principles for such funds are generally the same as business accounting principles.

Enterprise fund—This is essentially the fund where ongoing activities operated like a business are recorded. Public utilities financed by user charges are a good example. Proceeds from revenue bond issues, and their disposition, are usually accounted for here.

Internal service funds—This fund accounts for goods or services that are provided by one part of the government to another part at cost. Central purchasing and parking facilities are examples of such services.

Fiduciary funds—These are *Trust and Agency Funds.* They account for money or property that is being held by the governmental unit as a trustee, guardian or agent for individuals, government entities, and nonpublic organizations. Pension funds, for example, are recorded here.

CASH vs. ACCRUAL BASIS OF ACCOUNTING

One of the major sources of controversy in government accounting is when to record expenditures and revenues. Businesses account on an accrual basis. Revenues are recorded when they are earned, not when the cash comes in. Expenses are recorded when they are incurred, not simply when the check is sent out. Some municipalities record revenues when the cash comes in and expenditures when the cash goes out. Some states even require this. Pure cash accounting can be confusing at best and misleading at worst, argue its critics.

The NCGA recommends what is called the modified accrual basis for governmental funds. Unlike a business, a government is not trying to measure expenses against sales. Rather, it is concerned with a different kind of matching. The NCGA suggests that revenues be recognized when they are available and measurable. Expenditures should be recognized when the liability is incurred. Interest and principal payments on debt should be recorded only when the payment is due, however. For proprietary funds, the full accrual method is recommended. Revenues, according to the NCGA, should be recorded when they are earned and expenses when they are incurred, just as in business. Fiduciary funds adopt the modified accrual or accrual method, depending on the type of fund.

BUDGETING

Budgeting is the primary means of financial management and control for governments. All fifty states require that operating budgets be in balance. The NCGA recommends that budgets be drawn up annually for all governmental funds. Comparison between actual and budgeted revenues and expenditures should be presented with the financial statements. Proprietary funds, which are treated like businesses, require less rigid budgets, says the NCGA.

FIXED ASSETS AND LONG-TERM LIABILITIES

General fixed assets and long-term liabilities are recorded in account groups that are separate from the funds themselves because, reasons the NCGA, they do not relate specifically to any one fund. The fixed assets associated with proprietary and trust funds, however, should be recorded in the respective funds. Depreciation, again because these operations are similar to businesses, is charged against those fixed assets in the proprietary funds and some trust funds. All other fixed assets are recorded in the General Fixed Assets Account Group at the cost of the purchase or construction. Depreciation is not charged against the assets.

The long-term liabilities of the special assessment fund, as well as the proprietary and trust funds, are recorded in those funds, respectively. Other long-term general obligation debt is recorded in the General Long-Term Debt Account Group.

FINANCIAL REPORTING

The NCGA recommends that governmental units should prepare both a comprehensive annual financial report and a more limited set of general purpose financial statements. The NCGA states that the general purpose financial statements are adequate for official statements, as well as for widespread distribution to those not interested in greater detail. The comprehensive annual financial report, however, is the official annual report. The NCGA also recommends that independent audits be undertaken of all state and local government financial statements.

The NCGA's recommended set of general purpose financial statements includes the following:

1—Combined balance sheet—all fund types and account groups.

2—Combined statement of revenues, expenditures, and changes in fund balances—all governmental fund types.

3—Combined statement of revenues, expenditures, and changes in fund balances—budget and actual—general and special revenue fund types (and similar governmental fund types for which annual budgets have been legally adopted).

4—Combined statement of revenues, expenses, and changes in retained earnings (or equity)—all proprietary fund types.

5—Combined statement of changes in financial position—all proprietary fund types.

6—Notes to the financial statements.

The NCGA recommends that the comprehensive annual financial report contain all these statements as well as considerably more detail. Separate funds within a given governmental fund should be itemized. Account group statements should be presented. Schedules of accounts receivable, investments, and other information can be presented. Statistical tables as well as certain introductory material such as the letter of transmittal should also be included. The NCGA lists in detail the material it recommends for both the comprehensive report and the general purpose statements in *Governmental Accounting and Financial Reporting Principles.*

Official Statement

The Municipal Finance Officers Association (MFOA) has actively encouraged state and local governments to adopt, voluntarily, guidelines for municipal disclosure in official statements that accompany new offerings. Basically, the MFOA believes the official statement should contain all information that could be pertinent to prospective investors. This includes the terms, features, and characteristics of the bonds, the legal authority for the bonds, the use of proceeds, and the financial health of the government or of the projects being financed. The financial information about a city would include outstanding debt, revenues, expenditures, budgets, and other liabilities, such as pension funds. A revenue issue would ideally include a detailed description of the finances of the project, as well as a listing and explanation of the protective covenants.

The cover page of an official statement gives a quick summary of the terms and features of the securities. The sample shown in Figure 3-5 indicates the information the MFOA recommends should appear on the cover page:*

1. The total principal amount of the securities.
2. The name of the issuer (with appropriate identification).
3. The type or title of issue being offered (e.g., general obligation, water revenue, etc.).
4. The date of the obligations, interest payment dates and the date from which interest is paid.
5. The denominations in which the securities are being offered.
6. Registration and exchange provisions.
7. Trustee and paying agents.
8. Redemption features, if any, including sinking fund provisions.
9. Maturity date and principal amount by maturity in columnar form.
10. A statement of the tax status of interest on the securities being offered.

---

*This can be found in the MFOA pamphlet *Disclosure Guidelines for Offerings of Securities by State and Local Governments.*

Additional information sometimes set forth on the cover page includes:

- Ratings by the various rating agencies.
- Designation as a new issue.
- Brief statement of the authority for issuance.
- Anticipated date and place of delivery.
- Summary statement of the security or source of payment.

FIGURE 3-5. Sample Cover Page from an Official Statement

---

① $78,815,000

② STATE OF MARYLAND

③ General Obligation Bonds

State and Local Facilities Loan of 1978—First Series

④ Interest will accrue from April 1, 1978 and will be payable October 1, 1978 and semi-annually thereafter on April 1 and October 1. The Bonds will be ⑤ issued as coupon Bonds in the denomination of $5,000 each, and such ⑥ coupon Bonds may be registered as to principal only, at the option and expense of the holder. Bonds which have been registered may be re-registered to bearer and thereafter transferred by delivery. The Bonds will be payable as to both principal and interest at the office of the State Fiscal ⑦ Agent, Mercantile-Safe Deposit & Trust Company, Baltimore, Maryland 21203.

---

⑧ The Bonds are not subject to redemption prior to their stated maturity.

The Bonds have been rated by *Moody's Investors Service, Inc.* as Aaa and by *Standard & Poor's Corporation* as AAA. See "Ratings" as to the bases, significance and possible effects of any changes, of the ratings.

In the opinion of Francis B. Burch, Attorney General of the State of Maryland, and of Messrs. O'Connor & Sweeney and Weinberg and Green, Bond Counsel, (i) the Bonds will be valid and legally binding general obligations of the State of Maryland to the payment of which the full faith and credit of the State are pledged; (ii) the Bonds, as property, and the ⑩ interest thereon, will be exempt from taxation by the State of Maryland and all its political subdivisions (however, interest on the Bonds will be includable in income of certain financial institutions in determining the amount of State franchise tax payable by them); and (iii) interest on the Bonds will be exempt from Federal income taxation under existing laws as now construed. See "Structure of State Debt" and "Tax Exemption."

---

(9) Amounts, Maturities, Coupon Rates and Yields or Prices

Series	Amount	Maturing April 1	Coupon Rate	Yield or Price
A	$4,460,000	1981	5.00%	4.10%
B	4,675,000	1982	5.00	4.15
C	4,895,000	1983	5.00	4.25
D	5,155,000	1984	4.70	4.35
E	5,415,000	1985	4.50	4.45
F	5,670,000	1986	4.50	100
G	5,965,000	1987	4.50	4.60
H	6,260,000	1988	4.70	4.65
I	6,570,000	1989	4.70	100
J	6,915,000	1990	4.70	4.75
K	7,240,000	1991	4.70	4.80
L	7,625,000	1992	4.70	4.85
M	7,970,000	1993	5.00	4.85

(accrued interest to be added)

The coupon rates shown above are the coupon rates payable by the State resulting from the successful bid for the Bonds on March 15, 1978 by a group of banks and investment banking firms. The yields or prices shown above were furnished by the successful bidders. Other information concerning the terms of the re-offering of the Bonds should be obtained from the successful bidders and not from the State of Maryland. See "Sale at Competitive Bidding."

Delivery of the Bonds is subject to the receipt of the approving opinions of the Attorney General of the State of Maryland and Bond Counsel, and other conditions specified in the Official Notice of Sale. It is expected that delivery of the Bonds in definitive form will be made in New York City on or about April 13, 1978.

March 15, 1978

The MFOA has established a Municipal Securities Information Document Central Repository which microfilms and files the financial statements of municipalities at no charge. Investors, underwriters, issuers, and other parties can subscribe to the service, which is run by Disclosure, Inc. They can also buy documents individually.

Insurance

In 1971, the American Municipal Bond Assurance Corp., a subsidiary of MGIC Investment Corp., was formed to write insurance on municipal bonds. The objective is to lower the interest cost to the issuer. For a one-time premium based on the total interest and principal of an issue, an issuer can insure the principal and interest payments on the bonds. The ultimate backing of the policies is the net worth of AMBAC, and in certain circumstances the additional net worth of the parent.

In 1974, Municipal Bond Insurance Association was established to insure municipal bonds. It is structured differently than AMBAC. The MBIA has five member underwriters: Aetna Casualty and Surety Co., Fireman's Fund Insurance Co., Aetna Insurance Co., Travelers Indemnity Co., and Continental Insurance Co. These five large firms are each liable for a fixed proportion of MBIA's insurance obligations. Premiums are based on the size of the principal and interest payments that can be paid by the issuer or the underwriter. Standard & Poor's rates both AMBAC-insured and MBIA-insured bonds as triple-A. Moody's ignores the insurance when assigning the rating. AMBAC will also issue bond portfolios of investors. (See Chapter 6.)

The question for the issuer is whether the interest cost on the bonds will be lowered by more than enough to make up for the premium payments. MBIA estimates that the issuers it insured in 1978 saved an average of 21 basis points a year in interest costs after the insurance premium was deducted.

4

How the Underwriter Works

The vast number of new municipal offerings each year, from every region of the country, has given rise to a large underwriting industry. There were some 1,800 dealers and dealer banks registered with the SEC in 1980. Probably about one-third of these are active. Many of the dealers are small, local underwriters who handle their communities' business. Even major issues in some states are mostly handled by local underwriters.

Nevertheless, as issues have grown larger and more complex, the major securities dealers and bank dealers in New York, Chicago, and on the West Coast have come to take the largest share of the business. The largest 25 firms, for example, managed more than 55 percent of the total volume of all new issues in 1980, according to statistics compiled by PSA. The growth in municipal bond business has meant that the municipal underwriting departments of the dealers and dealer banks have grown enormously. In fact, in the 1970s, municipal underwriting for some large securities firms was one of the two or three fastest-growing areas of the firms.

In principle, the underwriter's task is very straightforward. In a competitive offering, the underwriters bid against each other to buy the issuer's bonds and then reoffer them to investors. The profit is the difference, or spread, between what the bonds were bought for and the underwriters sell them for. In a negotiated offering, there is no bidding. The underwriter is chosen beforehand. But, in both cases, underwriters take complete risk and responsibility for selling the bonds, although the risk may be somewhat more limited for the underwriter in a negotiated offering.

Successful underwriting requires a trading and sales operation that knows the marketplace well and can reach prospective buyers quickly. Successful underwriters also generally have enough capital to take positions in issues if an underwriting is selling poorly. Still, for virtually any sizable issue, negotiated or competitive, underwriters will join together in a syndicate. The purpose is to spread the risk of the sale and to gain wider access to potential investors.

On a typical competitive issue, several syndicates of underwriters will bid against each other. The composition of the syndicates will vary from issue to issue. One co-manager might be a major national dealer or dealer bank, while the other might be a smaller dealer with a strong marketing organization in the region or state of the issuer. Another team might combine one manager that specializes in institutional sales with a so-called wire house that has a broad clientele of individual investors.

The procedures, rules, and technicalities involved in underwriting an issue are intricate and the pace is often very fast. Major underwriting firms may bid on ten or twelve issues a day and underwrite ten issues or more a week. The professionals in the business become adept at preparing quickly and making spur-of-the-moment decisions. Moreover, each underwriting generally involves the entire trading and sales operation of the firm.

The Notice of Sale

With the help of a financial advisor or underwriter the issuer will decide on how, when, and in what amount to issue bonds. In most states, general obligation bonds must be sold on a competitive basis by law. But sales of revenue issues are generally negotiated.

Financial advisors will occasionally act as the underwriter of an issue for which they are advisors. But the practice is becoming rare for large issues. The Municipal Securities Rulemaking Board has adopted Rule G-23 to address potential conflicts of interest in these relationships. G-23 requires that a financial advisor must terminate the advisory relationship or disclose possible conflicts of interest and compensation to be earned before acting as the underwriter on a negotiated issue. In competitive issues, the issuer must give its consent for the financial advisor to bid along with other underwriters.

If the issuer decides to sell its bonds on a negotiated basis, arrangements are made with the underwriters selected by the issuer. In competitive sales, advertisements are placed announcing the proposed sale, usually in local and national media. The traditional advertising document is termed the Official Notice of Sale. Active issuers will usually send the Notice of Sale to prospective bidders, as well as place it with their legal publications. An advertisement in the industry's national trade paper, *The Daily Bond Buyer,* is virtually a requirement for any significant issue. Industry members also recommend advertisements in the local community. Some states have their own municipal bond publications. The Notice should always include the following information:

1. Date, time, and place of sale.
2. Amount of issue, the maturity schedule and call features.
3. Authorization for the bond sale.
4. The type of bond (general obligation or type of revenue bond).
5. Interest payment dates.
6. Limitation on coupon rates.
7. Denominations of the bonds.
8. Registration privileges of investors.
9. Total amount of the bid at par or better (or discount allowed).
10. Required amount of good faith check.
11. Names of the bond counsel, and the statement of legality.
12. Basis for bidding, and method of award.
13. Method and place of settlement for the bonds.
14. Dating of the issue.
15. Statement of purpose of bonds, and security.
16. Bearer of printing, legal, and other expenses.
17. Statement of municipality's right to reject any or all bids.

Underwriting departments keep close track of new issues coming to market. *The Daily Bond Buyer* lists most significant negotiated and competitive issues in one of three sections: "Proposed New Issues," "Invitation for Bids," and "Official Municipal Bond Notices." *The Daily Bond Buyer* also offers a separate service that provides specific information about major new offerings, as well as worksheets that have become accepted industrywide to work out yields and prices for an issue. The service is available on a subscription basis and is called "New Issue Worksheet and Record Service." It also provides information on the offering yields of the other issues that have recently come to market.

Research and Sales

Banks and securities dealers typically begin their underwriting procedure with an opinion from their research staff. Many large firms restrict themselves to underwriting bonds with only high ratings. The rating agencies will be hired by issuers to analyze and rate most significant new issues. But underwriters also want an independent judgment on the quality of an issue, and a more precise sense of how the issue compares to other issues with the same or similar ratings. If an analyst is particularly confident about the financial health of a municipality, the underwriters might make a more aggressive bid. If the analyst feels disclosure is inadequate or the bonds are too risky, the firm may not bid at all.

The sales force of the underwriters is usually informed each week regarding upcoming bond issues. A typical procedure is to hold a Monday morning meeting with sales people or managers and go over each new issue of the week. The research concerning the issues will then be discussed, as will the underwriters' and traders' sense of how yields in the overall market will trade. A preliminary strategy is then established and the sales force seeks prospective buyers. As noted, underwriters argue that the salesmen work far better on a negotiated issue because they are certain that their firm will be underwriting it.

The Syndicate

Well before the week of the bond sale, the underwriters form their buying syndicates. In most cases, this is perfunctory. History rules, by and large. Traditionally, the underwriter will stay with the group bid with the last time the particular municipality came to market. The managers usually retain their position also. For smaller issues, one dealer may underwrite the entire offering.

The composition of syndicates can change, of course. Firms go out of business and new ones are started. Others may simply want to drop out of the syndicate.

Syndicates in municipal bonds can have only two members or as many as 100 members or more. There can be one manager or several co-managers, although only one of them—the "senior" or "lead" manager—actually "runs the books of the account."

The syndicate members are bound together for any issue by the syndicate letter or contract. The letter contains the terms under which the account will be managed, including the obligations of all the members. The manager sends the letter to each member of the account typically two weeks before the issue is to be sold. The members must sign and return it if the terms are agreed on. The letters vary, but they generally include the following contents.

1. The amount of bonds to be underwritten by each member (the participations).
2. Duration of the account.
3. That the bid and offering terms will be set by the majority of the members.
4. The obligations of members as to expenses, the good faith deposit, and the liability for any unsold bonds.
5. Appointment of the manager as agent for the account.
6. Granting of rights to the syndicate manager, including borrowing, advertising, the pledging of securities, and making the bid.
7. Granting unspecified authority to the manager where necessary to perform the functions properly.
8. A provision that no liability is assumed by the manager except for lack of good faith.
9. The priority of orders.

EASTERN AND WESTERN ACCOUNTS

There are two types of syndicate accounts that predominate in different parts of the country. The Eastern account is generally used in the major financial centers of the East and West Coasts. The Eastern account is undivided as to sales and liability. The members of these accounts pool the bonds they have to sell as well as the liability for any unsold bonds. Undivided as to sales means syndicate members can sell any of the bonds in an account as long as they are available. But the syndicate profits are divided according to participations agreed to before the sale, no matter how many bonds any individual member sells. Undivided as to liability means that, if any bonds cannot be sold, all members are liable for a proportionate share of those bonds according to the same participations.

A member, for example, might have a 10 percent participation in an account. If the member sells only 5 percent of the bonds, the member is still entitled to 10 percent of the syndicate's net underwriting profits. On the other hand, even though the member may sell more than 10 percent of the bonds, the syndicate may not be able to sell the whole issue. The member is liable for 10 percent of the unsold bonds despite the sales made, and the member would still receive only 10 percent of the net underwriting profits. To repeat, members can sell any of the bonds as long as they have not already been sold. The managers usually take the largest participations. The next tier of members will take a smaller participation, and so on.

In Western, or divided accounts, which predominate throughout the center of the country, members of the account are assigned a portion of each of several groups of bonds. The bonds, for example, might be broken down into several brackets of different maturities. But the account is divided only as to liability, not as to sales. A member firm can sell any of the bonds in the issue, according to a priority that is discussed later. This is similar to the Eastern account. But the member is only liable for any unsold bonds if the member firm has not sold its full participation in each bracket. Sometimes, some maturities in a given offering are sold on a completely undivided basis, while others are sold on a divided basis.

It should be emphasized that the net underwriting profits of the syndicate are by no means the only revenues that the member firms can earn. Syndicate members receive discounts, known as concessions and takedowns, on bonds they sell or take for their own inventory. If the member can sell the bond for the offering price or at a small discount, the remainder is kept as the firm's revenues. This is discussed more fully later in this chapter.

Competitive Sales

Once the syndicate is formed, the requirements are in place to make the bid. A day or two before the bid must be placed, a preliminary price meeting of the members of the syndicate is held. In New York City and several other large cities, the members usually meet at the manager's office. Throughout the rest of the country, price meetings are usually set up by the manager over the phone with the various account members. When syndicates are very large, managers often use the Munifacts wire, a service of the Bond Buyer, to transmit information to members. Munifacts is the principal news wire that serves the municipal industry, but it also has a service that can communicate information only to specified clients if desired. Most dealers subscribe to the Munifacts wire.

The preliminary meetings are comparatively relaxed. The dealer members are usually represented by one of the two or three members of the syndicate group of the firm. He or she consults with the firm's traders and salesmen on the day of the meeting to see what potential there is in the market, how other comparable issues have gone, and so on. He or she will typically enter the proposed prices or yields for each maturity of the issue, called the reoffering scale, onto the Bond Buyer worksheets.

The managers run the price meetings. They will ask for each member's proposed scale, reading off their own preliminary ideas as well. They will possibly discuss the spread for the underwriters. There is seldom much argument at the preliminary meetings, and a consensus is often reached easily. The goal is to come up with the highest bid to the issuer, that is, the lowest interest rate, and still be confident of selling the bonds at a profitable spread. A preliminary scale is set and salesmen solicit orders.

The final price meeting is usually set an hour before the time the bid is due. The manager is responsible for setting up the procedure for delivering the sealed bid by the deadline. The deadline is very strictly adhered to, and most bids must be delivered by hand. Underwriters will usually arrange for a local dealer or bank to send someone with the bid to the municipality. The municipality determines how the bid should be computed. See the Appendix for the alternative computations.

The manager must also send the municipality a good faith check on the day of the bid. This is to be used in case the underwriter does not deliver the proceeds of the sale as agreed on. The check is usually about 2 percent of the total amount of the bonds to be issued.

The final price meetings can be very tense. The individual members again go over the scales with their traders and salesmen beforehand. By the day of the bid, some orders for bonds are often lined up. What adds to the tension of a price meeting is that the bid must be placed within an hour, and the winner will be known only a few minutes after the deadline. Traditionally, the competing syndicates tell each other their bids just after the deadline.

TYPES OF ORDERS

A complete understanding of the several types of orders and their pricing is important. The highest-priced order is sold to investors at the net—that is, the price or yield actually shown in the reoffering scale. These prices are always the ones agreed to by the syndicate. The underwriting group retains the full spread.

But generally the underwriting group will give up part of their spread to get orders from dealers who are not in the syndicate. These dealers are offered what is known as a concession. A typical spread might be $10 per $1,000 bond (one point). The concession might be $2.50 (1/4 point). A municipal dealer with a municipal bond department is entitled to that $2.50 discount, enabling it to buy the bonds for $997.50 and sell them to a customer for the full $1,000, retaining the $2.50. The bonds are said to be bought "at the concession."

Individual members of the syndicate can buy the bonds "at the takedown" for their own account, for sale to another dealer, or for sale directly to an investor. The takedown might amount to an additional $2.50 on top of the concession, the total takedown coming to $5.00. So the syndicate member can buy the bonds at $995 and sell them to a dealer outside the group for $997.50 who, in turn, can sell them for $1,000. In this case, the member would keep only the $2.50 for compensation. If sold at the net price to an investor, the member would keep the full $5.00 takedown.

The prices and priorities of the several types of orders are a critical part of an underwriting. If an offering is oversubscribed, low-priority orders may not get filled. According to Rule G-11 of the MSRB, the priority of orders must be furnished in writing to all syndicate members. The traditional types of orders, in priority order, follow:

Pre-sale orders—The orders made before the syndicate actually offers the bonds. These orders can be made at a net price, concession, or takedown. They usually have first priority over the other orders made at these prices.

Group net orders—The orders made once the offering is under way at a net price. Again, the spread goes to the profit of the whole syndicate.

Group orders less the concession—Purchases by dealers who are not members of the syndicate but are entitled to the concession. The remainder of the spread accrues to the whole syndicate.

Designated orders—Sales to investors at the net price where the concession (and sometimes the takedown) is designated by the investor to be retained by two or more members of the account.

Member orders—Purchases by members at the takedown for their own account or for sale to another dealer or investor. The account member keeps the full takedown if the bonds are sold to the investor, or reallows the concession if the sale is made to a dealer.

Should the offering be oversubscribed, the first orders to be filled are the pre-sale net orders and group net orders. The last orders to be filled are the member orders. Investors might prefer to enter group orders rather than net designated or member orders to be more certain that they will receive their bonds. An order is seldom confirmed until the order period is over.

FINAL PRICE MEETING

The final price meeting usually begins with the manager giving the proposed scale. He or she might also suggest the size of the spread. If any sales have been made or lined up already, they are announced. The manager might also fill in members on the latest developments in the marketplace. The yields on other issues for sale that day are watched closely as benchmarks for determining yields on the issue being under-written. Then the manager polls the members for their opinions about the scales and the spread.

As the members read off their scales, disagreements arise. They will center on the yields for particular maturities or the size of the spread. A member can drop out of the syndicate at any time before the bid is placed.

During the price meeting, orders will typically be coming in. The trading and sales departments of the member firms are working to line up sales and they call their representatives at the meeting immediately on receiving an order. In an offering that is going well, some maturities may sell out before the meeting is over. As orders come in, the members can start edging their bid up by lowering the yield on some maturities. If few orders come in, the group may get more cautious and raise yields.

As the price meeting continues, an idea of where demand is strong or weak develops and the scale falls into place. Sometimes, the members believe the spread is too small and will try to get the manager to widen it.

Occasionally, a compromise will be struck where the spread will be widened but yields on some maturities are reduced. Generally, the manager wields the most influence at the price meetings, but a big order from a member can force a sudden adjustment in the scale. The order period is set at the final price meeting. It usually will run for one or two hours.

A few minutes before the deadline, the final scale is sent to the computer, where the bid will be calculated almost instantaneously. The bid is then telephoned to the person who will deliver it to the municipality. If the syndicate wins, the members work immediately to sell out the entire issue. If the issue, or certain maturities of the issue, are indeed oversubscribed, allotments will be made according to the priority of orders, as stated above. If a given level of priority bonds are oversubscribed, bonds are allotted to members of the syndicate on a pro rata basis according to their underwriter participation.

MSRB Rule G-11 requires that the procedure for changing the priority of orders, and any permission for the syndicate manager to allot orders in any way other than by the agreed priority, be furnished in writing by the manager to syndicate members prior to the first offer of securities by the syndicate. In addition, any changes in priority not previously agreed to must be furnished by the manager in writing to members. If orders can be confirmed prior to the end of the order period, that information too must be furnished in writing to members beforehand. According to Rule G-11 (g), the senior syndicate manager, within ten business days from the date of sale, must disclose to other members of the syndicate, in writing, a summary statement identifying the allocation of securities to orders which, under the priority provisions, were entitled to a higher priority than a member's "take down" order.

. Rule G-8 of the MSRB regarding record keeping requires the manager of the syndicate to maintain the records of the account. The records must include a description and the aggregate par value of the bonds, the name and percentage participation of each member, the terms and conditions governing the syndicate, all orders received for securities from the syndicate, all allotments of securities and their prices, the date and amount of the good faith deposit, the date of settlement and of the account closing, and a reconciliation of profits and expenses.

Orders are usually confirmed by telephone by the manager of the account when the order period is over. But only issues in the greatest demand are typically sold out within the one or two hours of the order period. Afterward, orders are taken from members on a first-come, first-served basis, regardless of the type of order. When the issue is sold out, the syndicate is disbanded.

Most syndicate accounts are set up to run for thirty days. They can then be renewed by the members if necessary. But very few new offerings are held open for that long. When an issue proves difficult to sell, the terms of the offering are often changed. Changing terms usually requires the majority consent of the members, with votes weighted by the participations of the members.

If the issue still cannot be sold, the bonds can be distributed among the members to try to sell. Or they can be given to a bond broker. All the remaining bonds can be given to one broker, or they can be split up in groups—according to maturity, for example—and given to one broker or several brokers. The broker then "puts the bonds out for the bid." Members can also bid for the bonds, as can any other dealer. Whoever produces the best bid for the group of bonds will win them, although the manager always retains the right to reject all bids. Brokers usually get 1/8th of a point ($1.25 per bond) as a commission for the transaction.

Negotiated Sales

Once the bidding is over, competitive and negotiated sales are very similar, although the pace is less frantic for negotiated sales. Usually, there is a preliminary pricing which may be revised upward or downward, depending on the degree of success of the presale order period. Final prices are set by the managers and members on the day of sale.

Another difference is that the public finance department is closely involved with the underwriting. As the number of negotiated offerings has grown in recent years, the size of the public finance departments has grown as well. On negotiated sales, it is the public finance group that usually maintains contact with the issuer. However, the syndicate department generally is still in charge of pricing the issue.

Managers' fees and expenses are handled somewhat differently for negotiated sales as well. A typical management fee is 20 percent of the spread in a negotiated sale, and is allocated by the managers among themselves. An allowance for various expenses is also agreed on beforehand with the issuer.

After the Sale

After the issue is sold, the manager of the syndicate must undertake a number of procedures to confirm orders, deliver and pay for the bonds and meet legal requirements. MSRB Rule G-12, the Board's Uniform Practice Code, details the procedures for confirming orders to members in an underwriting. All sales of new issues are made on a when, as and if issued basis. Written confirmations for when, as and if issued orders must generally be sent within two business days after the trade date, according to G-12 (c) (iii). G-12 (c) (v) sets forth the information requirements for each confirmation to a dealer. G-15 (a) establishes the requirements for confirmations to a non-dealer or non-broker customer. The requirements are listed in Chapter 5.

Just after the issue is sold, the senior manager sends a letter to all members of the account that states the terms for the issue. The letter will include the reoffering terms of the issue, including the spread, takedown, and concession, as well as confirm the price to be paid to the issuer. It will also announce whether and how the issue will be advertised in the financial press, list the participations of the members in a competitive sale, and can include other information as well. The members must sign and return the letter. In most advertisements, the members of the account are listed in the order of the size of their participations.

Before or at the time customers are sent their final written confirmations, Rule G-32 of the MSRB requires that the underwriter send them a copy of the official statement for the issue or an abstract or summary of the official statement if available. In negotiated sales, information on underwriting spreads, fees and the offering price for each maturity must also be sent to customers.

It generally takes about one month from the sale before the bonds are actually ready to be delivered to investors. This allows time for printing the bonds, and for the bond counsel to prepare the final opinion and transcript of proceedings. Up to that point, bond counsel has given only a preliminary opinion, and the sale of the bonds is conditional on the final opinion. The opinion is usually printed on the back of the bonds. The transcript generally includes a certificate stating that there is no litigation pending against the bonds and a guarantee of the signatures of the officials who signed the bonds, among other documents.

When the bonds are finally delivered to the senior manager, they must be paid for. The manager will borrow the money from a bank, usually a member of the syndicate. If the manager is a bank, it will finance the loan itself. The payment is made less the amount of the good faith check. In turn, the bonds are delivered to the members of the account according to the allotments. The members then pay off their share of the sales. As the payments come in, the manager pays off the loan, usually within a few days. According to G-12 (c) (iii), the manager must furnish a written confirmation of orders as well as notification of the settlement date to members six business days before the settlement date. The settlement date is the date on which the bonds are delivered and paid for.

Once the bonds are paid for, the senior manager will distribute the profits to members of the account. If there was a loss on the underwriting, the members are assessed for their share. The distribution is accompanied by a final statement of the participations, expenses, and profits of the syndicate. Rule G-11 (h) requires that the manager make known all expenses to account members. According to G-12 (j), syndicates must be settled within sixty days after bonds have been delivered.

Because it generally takes a month for the bonds to be delivered, investors are not entitled to the full six months of interest for the first payment period. They have not put up their money on the date when interest first starts accruing, the dated date, nor have the municipalities had use of the proceeds. As pointed out in Chapter 1, the investor must pay the accrued interest to the seller—in this case, the issuer. The investor then receives the full six months of interest on the interest payment date. Dealers will simply add on the accrued interest to the price of the bonds.

5

The Secondary Market

Few modern markets for new issues of securities can function well
without the support of a secondary market where those securities can be
traded after they are first sold. Investors will pay a better price for a new
issue if they know that the security can be sold at a fair price before its
maturity. The best-known secondary markets are for corporate equities,
and for good reason. Because stocks are not redeemed at a specific date,
investors need a secondary market in order to convert their investments
to cash. Bondholders, by contrast, expect to receive their cash on maturity.
Still, bondholders want the opportunity to be able to sell their securities
before they mature.

Aside from supporting the primary market, a thriving secondary market
also serves investors by providing them with an array of different types of
securities to suit their needs, and a way to buy and sell quickly when
necessary. That makes a variety of investing strategies with different risks
and maturities possible.

The size of the secondary market in municipal securities is hard to
determine. Unlike the corporate market, almost no trading is done on
any exchange. Nor is there a computerized marketplace designed to
capture at least a significant number of the trades. *The Blue List* typically
lists 12,000 municipal issues a day worth $1 billion. Not all the bonds
by any means are traded every day. Observers generally estimate that
secondary market trading comes to between one and two times the volume
in the primary market. Since some $76 billion in new issues came to market
in 1980, the secondary market may have traded as much as $152 billion
of securities, or more.

Investors sell municipal securities before maturity for many reasons. Individual or institutional investors may need cash, new heirs may want to sell, the outlook for interest rates may change, the perception of credit quality of securities may change, the profitability of corporate investors may fall. Investors may simply see better opportunities elsewhere in the marketplace.

When they do sell, investors may get more or less for the bonds than they originally paid, depending on two major factors. First, if the general level of municipal interest rates has changed from the date the bonds were bought, the resale value of those bonds will also shift. If interest rates are currently higher than they were for the bonds the investor bought, the bonds will be worth less. If interest rates have declined, the bonds are worth more. The potential price fluctuations due to changes in the general level of municipal rates are termed the market risk.

The second factor has to do with the individual issue and issuer, the credit risk. If the credit of the issuer improves, the bond would be worth more. If the credit weakens, the bonds will fall in value. In an extreme case, some New York City issues fell in price by thirty and forty points and more in the wake of the financial crisis of 1975. More likely is a smaller shift in the credit worthiness of certain issuers that often results in a change in ratings by the rating agencies.

Municipal bond traders of dealer firms and dealer banks are the principal market makers in the secondary market. Working at a telephone console throughout each day, they buy from and sell to other dealers, investors, and for their own inventory. Municipal bond traders must have a sense of what kinds of bonds clients might want and not get caught with an inventory that is hard to sell, especially when interest rates are rising. It is a fast-paced and risky business activity.

Distinct Features of Municipal Bond Trading

There are several characteristics of municipal bond trading that make it very different from most other securities trading. Most municipal bonds are traded on the basis of yield, all trades are done over-the-counter, and there are no set trading hours. Moreover, as noted in Chapter 1, almost all transactions are principal or dealer transactions. That means, firms generally do not act as brokers between two parties trading municipal securities, which is the way corporate stocks are often traded. Rather, municipal bonds are usually sold out of a firm's inventory. The profit to the firm is the markup above the cost to the dealer when it is sold to the investor. Municipal securities, then, are sold just like goods off the shelf. A typical markup, or spread, is about $10 a bond. But it can often be higher, sometimes as high as $40 or more—in the case of a bond that does not trade frequently, or one that involves high risk.

Probably the most significant distinction in municipal bond trading, as noted in Chapter 1, is the vast number of issues that must be kept track of. The inevitable result is that the market for many smaller issues is thin, and therefore involves higher spreads.

The number of issues handicaps the municipal trader in an important way compared to counterparts in other markets. To reduce risk, and to be able to shift strategies quickly, traders of most kinds of securities are able to maintain short positions. That is, they borrow and then sell securities they do not own in anticipation that prices will fall, or to hedge against purchases of other securities. If prices do fall, they buy back the securities they sold short, earning a profit. They return the securities to the lender with interest. By going short, these dealers are able to hedge themselves against a decline in securities prices.

Because there are so many municipal issues, so many of which are small, it is often hard to find owners from whom to borrow the securities. The municipal traders, as a result, can seldom go short to the degree traders in other securities do. This limits the trader's ability to take large positions in securities because he or she can't be protected in the event that the market turns downward. They can use the Treasury bond futures market for some measure of protection, even though it seldom provides a perfect hedge. Municipal traders do sell short frequently, however, in dollar bond, note and "when, as and if issued" markets where there is a large supply of outstanding securities.

Securities dealers—The municipal trading departments of full-service securities firms will generally provide service to both investors and other dealers. These traders will make markets in a variety of securities, maintaining large inventories. In securities firms with many branch offices, the sales liaison staff plays an important role. These liaison personnel usually sit near the traders, and are assigned to specific sales offices. Account executives in these offices will place their orders through the liaison staff.

Dealer banks—Commercial banks that actively underwrite municipal bonds also generally maintain sizable trading operations. Just as they cannot underwrite many revenue bonds, they also cannot trade in them in the secondary market as principals. They can, however, buy and sell revenue bonds on an agency basis. Dealer banks actively make markets in general obligation bonds. However, the trading department cannot execute transactions for the trust department of the bank that buys bonds for its individual trust accounts.

Brokers' brokers—The relative handful of brokers, mostly located in New York, only trade for dealers. Some of them maintain elaborate trading operations, and others specialize in certain types of securities. They act as agents, not as principals, and do not carry inventories of bonds, and charge a broker's commission. Their role is discussed further later in this chapter.

A typical dealer trading department will have people specializing in various kinds of bonds. Almost all trading operations of any size have one trader who specializes in dollar bonds. Some of the more active and competitive trading goes on in these securities because the issues are usually large and create a lot of institutional investor interest. Firms frequently also maintain a specialist in the trading of notes. Here again, trading is more active than in most other municipal securities. Notes appeal principally to financial institutions and typically trade in large denominations.

Trading departments can vary in their emphasis. Some firms have specialists in odd lots of bonds, usually trades of $25,000 or less. A round lot in municipal trading is generally $100,000, although some firms consider it to be higher. Local issues are often the province of one trader on the desk. Some firms, for example, have one person trading in New York City issues. Trading operations with broader geographical territories may divide their trading staff by region. With the rise in the number of housing revenue bonds, some traders will concentrate in this area. Some large securities dealers maintain small trading staffs in various national sales offices where municipal bond business is particularly active. For most issues, trading decisions in these offices are often made independently of headquarters, although some firms refer very large trades to the main office. A handful of Chicago and West Coast banks keep underwriting and trading operations offices in New York City.

Sources of Information

Aside from the municipal bond traders' own contacts with the marketplace, there are several important sources of information that are available.

THE BLUE LIST

Perhaps the most widely available trading information in the market, and one of the oldest, is *The Blue List*. Distributed nationally every morning by Standard & Poor's, it lists securities and yields or prices of bonds being offered by dealers. Recently, *The Blue List* has been computerized, enabling participating dealers to retrieve current information throughout the day. Dealers do not have to wait until the next morning to see what offerings have been added to, or deleted from, the list. The changes appear immediately on a computer screen—the Blue List Ticker —for subscribers to the service.

MUNICIPAL DEALER OFFERING SHEETS

Most municipal bond dealers will publish a list of bonds in their inventory that they are willing to sell, along with offering yields or prices. Such lists are usually made available to other dealers and the firm's investors as often as they are published. Typically, dealers publish a list weekly. Sometimes these lists are also fed to *The Blue List*.

MUNIFACTS WIRE

Aside from its regular news and underwriting services, Munifacts, run by *The Bond Buyer,* carries offerings of securities with yields and concessions on their wire. Dealers phone in their offerings and they will appear on the wire for all subscribers.

THE KENNY WIRE AND THE C-WIRE

J. J. Kenny & Co., the largest municipal bond broker, has developed a computerized wire service that reaches some 600 or more dealers. While it carries other information on the wire, its bread-and-butter activity is to list bonds for which bids are being sought by dealers. A wire competitive with the Kenny wire was started in 1978 by Chapdelaine & Co., also in New York. It is called the C-Wire.

THE BOND BUYER PLACEMENT RATIO AND VISIBLE SUPPLY

The Bond Buyer publishes two measures daily that are widely followed in the industry. The placement ratio (Figure 5-1) is that proportion of all competitive and negotiated issues over $1 million that were distributed during the week. It is a good indicator of the demand for securities among investors. Since 1951, when it was initiated, the ratio's high was 99.4 percent and its low was 29.2 percent.

The 30-day visible-supply volume (Figure 5-2) is the measure of all offerings scheduled to come to market in the next 30 calendar days. It is an indication of expected supply in the new issue market. *The Bond Buyer* breaks the numbers down between competitive and negotiated issues. They are derived from the columns entitled Sealed Bids Invited for Competitive Issues and Proposed Bond Issues for Negotiated Offerings that appear in *The Bond Buyer* on a daily basis.

BOND INDEXES

The most widely watched municipal bond indexes are two compiled by *The Bond Buyer*. Both *The Bond Buyer* indexes are composed of dealers' estimates, gathered weekly by *The Bond Buyer,* of the yield that a hypothetical 20-year bond would have to carry if that issue came to market during the week. The 20-bond index includes 20 actual issuers. The average of the ratings of these issuers falls midway between Moody's top four ratings. The 11-bond index is composed of 11 of the 20 issuers in the first average, but the quality rating averages a solid "Aa" from Moody's. Dow Jones & Co. also issues a weekly average based on 20-year maturities. There are 20 seasoned issues in the average. Dow Jones asks dealers to estimate the yields on those actual issues if they were to mature in 20 years.

None of these three averages includes any revenue bonds. The Dow Jones average, in addition, contains only relatively low-coupon bonds because they are older issues.

The Bond Buyer recently began computing a separate index based on 30-year revenue bonds. The new index includes 25 issuers of revenue bonds for a variety of purposes, including housing, transportation, hospitals, and pollution control. The ratings on the bonds included in the index range from Moody's "Aaa" to "Baa" and from Standard & Poor's "AAA" to "A."

FIGURE 5-1. Placement Ratio

- The Bond Buyer Placement Ratio is compiled weekly as of the close of business Thursday. The Ratio represents the amount of bonds distributed weekly as a percentage of each week's new Issue accounts of $1 million or more. Since it was started on Feb. 15, 1951, the highest percentage was recorded on July 19, 1951, at 99.4%, and the lowest on Nov. 23, 1960, at 29.2%.

  The figures shown below are as of the first Thursday in each month except that in the current month and that immediately preceding, they are shown weekly.

Also shown are the highs and lows for the last 5 years.

	No. New Accts.	Total Amt. New Accts. $	Sales from New Accts. $	Placement Ratio %
1980		(000 omitted)		
6/ 5	58	1,536,209	1,431,504	93.2
5/29	52	799,061	559,651	70.0
5/22	60	1,015,635	931,895	91.8
5/15	57	1,092,755	1,004,875	92.0
5/ 8	53	942,504	873,339	92.7
5/ 1	54	1,201,369	1,176,980	98.0
4/ 3	24	225,053	209,488	93.1
3/ 6	22	492,627	474,423	96.3
2/ 7	45	433,599	363,249	83.8
1/ 3	1	1,100	910	82.7

	High		Low	
1980	98.0%	(5/ 1)	82.7%	(1/ 3)
1979	98.1%	(11/29)	76.0%	(4/12)
1978	96.3%	(9/14)	73.4%	(3/ 2)
1977	95.5%	(10/27)	58.4%	(1/ 6)
1976	93.8%	(11/18)	65.1%	(1/15)

SOURCE: The Daily Bond Buyer

Individual dealers will sometimes compile their own averages to focus on a specific part of the municipal market. One dealer, for example, compiles separate indexes on housing, utility, pollution control, and hospital bonds.

WHITE'S TAX-EXEMPT BOND MARKET RATINGS

In the diverse municipal market, the White's Ratings rank where the yields for 20-year bonds of some 37,000 issuers would fall in relation-

FIGURE 5-2. Visible Supply of Municipals

● The 30-Day Visible Supply is compiled each day from our columns "Sealed Bids Invited" for competitive offerings and "Proposed Bond Issues" for negotiated transactions and reflects the total dollar volume of bonds anticipated to reach the market over the next 30 days. Beginning in 1971 a total of negotiated offerings is compiled daily. It does not include short-term notes. The expected total appears daily in "Municipal Dollar Bowrs" under Market Indicators. Since its compilation was started in Dec., 1927 peak volume for competitive offerings was recorded on May 10, 1976, at $2,175,290,089 bonds and low on March 3, 1943 at $928,000.

The figures shown below are of the first Friday in each month, except those in the current month and the month immediately preceding which are shown as of every Friday. Also shown are the highs and lows for the last 5 years.

1980	Competitive $	Negotiated $	Total $
6/ 6	1,359,239,000	721,260,000	2,080,499,000
5/30	1,781,512,030	1,070,260,000	2,851,772,030
5/23	1,824,677,366	736,825,000	2,561,502,366
5/16	1,461,401,090	781,360,000	2,242,761,090
5/ 9	1,104,498,788	1,104,175,000	2,208,673,788
5/ 2	572,273,745	635,745,000	1,208,018,745
4/ 3	912,051,000	409,515,000	1,321,566,000
3/ 7	1,085,006,434	940,045,000	2,025,051,434
2/ 1	781,715,600	555,300,000	1,337,015,600
1/ 4	977,894,399	444,350,000	1,422,244,399

	High		Low	
1980	$1,824,677,366	(5/23)	$449,974,100	(3/20)
1979	$2,037,523,810	(10/ 8)	$189,035,000	(12/20)
1978	$1,751,956,000	(4/24)	$311,320,920	(8/22)
1977	$1,693,105,735	(6/ 3)	$458,103,797	(8/24)
1976	$2,175,290,089	(5/10)	$498,374,012	(12/ 9)

(Highs and lows are for competitive offerings only.)

SOURCE: The Daily Bond Buyer

ship to each other. A very secure bond is assigned the benchmark number 100. A bond that the service believes would trade .05 percent in yield higher would be assigned a rating of 99. Each .05 percent increment higher pushes the rating one point lower.

Each week, White's Ratings publishes in *The Blue List* the rate that the benchmark 100 is equal to. If 100 equaled 5.80 percent one week, a bond with a rating of 90 should trade around 6.30 percent, a .05 percent rise for every point below 100. White's Ratings is published once a year.

The Trading

Probably the most important sources of information to the bond trader, however, are his or her own contacts, and those of the salesmen. Traders will try to develop a knowledge of who has what bonds and at what price they may be willing to sell them. He or she will also want a sense of where demand for bonds might be strong, and what kinds of issues will be most sought after. Trading desks and bond brokers will frequently keep an account of the amount held by customers in certain actively traded issues.

The goal of the trading department is to turn over its inventory quickly and profitably. Carrying inventory too long is expensive because it ties up costly capital that could be used elsewhere. Dealers usually borrow to finance their inventories. Holding securities is always a risk if interest rates turn upward quickly. Prices must then be marked down. To spread risk, dealers often take large positions in conjunction with other dealers. This "joint account" enables dealers to service large investors without being locked into unwieldy positions.

Trading conforms to the normal bid and ask procedure in all over-the-counter markets. The listing of the yield is always the offering side of the market. Investors may not care to buy the bonds for that yield and may bid at a lower price—that is, a higher yield. A bid of 6.40 percent and an ask of 6.25 percent means a dealer is willing to buy the bonds at 6.40 percent and to sell them at 6.25 percent.

Typically, the description of the bonds in a verbal transaction includes the agreed yield or price less a concession, if any, the par value amount of bonds, the name of the bonds, the coupon rate and maturity date. If bonds are callable, that should be made known to the buyer. Traders often go over the terms of a trade twice, and it is common for traders to call back immediately if there is any doubt over the terms agreed upon.

Sometimes offerings are made on an all-or-none basis—an AON offering—where the offeror only agrees to sell the bonds if all that he has available will be bought. "Multiples of" offerings are also common, where sellers offer bonds only in lots of 25, 50, 100, or 200 bonds of $1,000 each.

A frequent practice in the industry is the option to buy—and, unlike with most securities, this option is free. The seller is asked to make a firm offering to the prospective buyer which will hold good for a stated time, say, a half hour. The bonds are said to be "out firm." The prospective buyer then has the option to get back to the seller and buy the bonds at the agreed-upon yield within the set time. If the buyer does not, the dealer can sell the bonds elsewhere. Occasionally, the option is accompanied by a recall privilege, which gives the seller the right to notify the buyer that he has only, say, five minutes left on the option. The amount of time is agreed on beforehand.

THE ROLE OF THE BROKERS' BROKERS

The bond brokers play a very significant role in the diverse secondary market. Bid-wanted business is probably the most common type of transaction for the broker. When dealers cannot or do not wish to obtain bids for bonds they want to sell, they may give them to a broker who will obtain bids from other dealers.

Brokers also work on any number of general "situations." Often, dealers will be looking to buy individual bonds or certain types of bonds. They may contact a broker to seek out those bonds. Dealers may have bonds to sell at a specific offering price, but do not want the whole dealer community to see them. A bond broker can isolate sectors of the market. As noted in the previous chapter, bond brokers are also called on to sell out what remains of an underwriting when the syndicate breaks up. Brokers do not release the identity of the dealers involved in transactions without their permission.

The advantage bond brokers have is their continuous communication with major dealers. The brokers track closely who owns and might want to buy or sell bonds, known as a "picture" of the market. The anonymity of the dealers makes them more willing to give bond brokers information. Often, the bond broker will have access to more information than a dealer will have. When brokers make a trade, they usually earn 1/8 of a point a bond, or $1.25. For high-volume trades, the commission is frequently cut.

MSRB Record-Keeping Rules

The MSRB has established several rules governing the record-keeping for holding securities and for transactions with customers. Rule G-8 is the basic record-keeping rule of the MSRB. G-8(a) (iii) requires that records be kept to show for each security, the long and short positions and the current location of the securities. Rule G-8(a) (ii) states that a separate record of all transactions undertaken with every customer must be kept. The account must contain "all purchases and sales of municipal securities, all receipts and deliveries of municipal securities, all receipts and disbursements of cash, and all other debits and credits relating to such account."

Also, records of each transaction, whether as a principal or agent, must be maintained according to Rules G-8(a) (vi) and (vii). Trading tickets will suffice for such records. They must show such information as the price and amount of the order, as well as the time of the execution "to the extent feasible." Other areas covered by Rule G-8 include the types of information to be obtained from customers, customer complaints, records for options, and several other categories. The record-keeping regulations by and large do not apply to dealers or brokers who do not do their own clearing, but Rule G-8 does provide that the non-clearing dealers and brokers remain responsible for accurate maintenance and preservation of the books and records.

Uniform Practices and Confirmation of Transactions

The MSRB has written rule G-12 to establish uniform practices among municipal bond dealers. Many of the rules are codifications of traditional practices that were adopted by firms prior to the establishment of the MSRB. Rule G-12 sets settlement dates, which are the dates on which bonds must be delivered and payment made. The settlement date is also the day used in computing yields and prices. For cash transactions, the settlement date is the day of the trade. For "regular way" transactions, the settlement date is the fifth business date after the trade date. For when, as and if issued transactions, usually new issues, the settlement date is as agreed between the parties, although it cannot be sooner than five business days after the final confirmation is out (six days for syndicate members).

The MSRB has also included under its uniform practice section requirements for confirmations of trades between dealers. Normally, a confirmation must be sent within one business day. For syndicate offerings, two business days are allowable, while cash transactions must be confirmed by telephone on the same day, and followed up with a written confirmation. Rule G-15 sets forth requirements for confirmations of transactions with non-dealer and non-broker customers. All such customers must receive a written confirmation "at or before the completion of a transaction." Most of the same information must be included both on dealer and on customer confirmations, but there are few differences. A summary of the requirements for dealer confirmations is in Rule G-12 (c) (v). Rule G-15 lists the following information as necessary for customer confirmations:

1. Name, address, and telephone number of the broker, dealer, or municipal securities dealer.
2. Name of customer.
3. Designation whether transaction was a purchase from or sale to the customer.
4. Description of the securities, including the issue name, interest rate, maturity date, whether securities are limited-tax, call feature, type of revenue bond, if such a bond, and the names of any obligors of the bonds.
5. Trade date and time of execution, or a statement that the time will be furnished upon request.
6. Settlement date.
7. Yield to maturity and resulting dollar price. If bonds are callable, the method of pricing must be stated, and a dollar price must be stated that is the lower of price to call or price to maturity.
8. Amount of accrued interest.
9. Extended principal amount.
10. Total dollar amount of transaction.
11. Whether the broker or dealer acted as a principal for its own account, an agent for the customer, an agent for someone else, an agent for both the customer and another party. (If the broker or dealer is acting for another party, the name or a promise to provide the name of the party is required, as is the amount of the remuneration to be received.)
12. A statement if delivery and payment of securities is any different than normal.

The MSRB also requests additional information if necessary to clarify an order. Such information might include the dated date, a statement about registration, or whether the securities are traded "flat" or "ex legal." Trading "flat" means without accrued interest, although all unpaid coupons are attached to the bonds. Ex legal means that a bond counsel's opinion is not attached.

Rule G-12 also covers several other important procedures. Verification of confirmations, delivery of securities and payment are dealt with at length. Practices are established for cases in which a buyer has reason to reject a security or the seller wishes to reclaim securities already delivered. A detailed procedure has also been established for closing out an order that has been confirmed but not completed.

6

The Investors

Commercial banks are the largest investors in municipal bonds. Of the approximately $326 billion of debt outstanding at the end of 1980, commercial banks held a little more than 46 percent, or $151.1 billion. Property and casualty insurance companies held $83.5 billion, or 25 percent, followed by households with 19 percent, or $62.9 billion.

Since the mid-1950s, these three categories of investors have dominated the municipal securities market. Nonfinancial corporations, as well as state and local governments, have been occasional buyers of the bonds. Life insurance companies, once substantial buyers, no longer invest significantly. Pension funds rarely buy because they are tax-exempt. Commercial banks, households, and casualty insurance companies accounted for approximately 90 percent of all bond purchases through the 1960s and 1970s.

The relative importance of each of the three major investors has shifted over the years. Through much of the 1960s, commercial banks absorbed two-thirds of all new municipal issues. In the 1970s, they took on less than one-third. Casualty insurance companies took up much of the slack, with some help from individual investors. The approval by Congress in 1976 of open-end bond funds gave individuals a new means of investing in municipal bonds. There were some $4.8 billion in these funds at the end of 1980. On balance, the municipal market is heavily institutional. By contrast, individuals own about two-thirds of all corporate stocks outstanding. (See Figure 6-1.)

FIGURE 6-1. Major Investors in State and Local Government Bonds

Percentage Share of Bonds Outstanding for Selected Years, 1955-1980

Year	% of Total Held by Households	% of Total Held by Commercial Banks	% of Total Held by Property and Casualty Insurance Companies
1955	42.2	28.2	9.1
1960	43.5	25.0	11.4
1965	36.3	38.7	11.3
1970	31.9	48.6	11.8
1975	30.4	46.0	14.9
1980	19.3	46.3	25.4

SOURCE: Federal Reserve Flow of Funds Accounts

The main attraction of municipal bonds to investors is obviously the tax exemption. The bond interest enjoys an exemption from all Federal income tax, as outlined in Chapter 1. State and local issues are also usually exempt from income taxes in their localities, although they are generally not exempt from taxes in other states.

Many municipal securities dealers supply investors with taxable yield equivalent tables like the one in Figure 1-2 to help them compute the benefit of tax-exempt yields to them. Where local taxes are high, dealers often have taxable yield equivalent tables that are adjusted for them as well. An abbreviated taxable equivalent table for New York City dwellers can be found in Figure 6-2.

The rule of thumb, as discussed in earlier chapters, is that investors in a tax bracket of 35 percent or higher will usually improve their after-tax return by investing in tax-exempt securities rather than taxable securities. Normally, tax-exempt rates trade at about 65 percent of rates on equivalent taxable securities. A tax-exempt bond paying 6 percent to the single investor in the 39 percent tax bracket would be worth a 9.84 percent yield if he or she had to pay taxes on it. This is no longer an unusually high marginal tax bracket. A married couple filing a joint return would reach the 32 percent bracket at a combined taxable income of about $25,000. Local taxes push tax brackets higher. For example, a taxable income of about $16,000 for residents of New York City filing a joint return would place them in the 32 percent bracket. If the couple

FIGURE 6-2. Tax Free Versus Taxable Income For New York State & New York City Residents

Combined Federal and New York State & New York City Tax Brackets 1980 Joint Taxable Income	Municipal Bond Yield (%)										
EQUIVALENT TAXABLE YIELD (%)	8.25	8.50	8.75	9.00	9.25	9.50	9.75	10.00	10.25	10.50	10.75
20,200-24,600 = 40.1%	13.77	14.19	14.61	15.03	15.44	15.86	16.28	16.69	17.11	17.53	17.95
24,600-29,900 = 44.4%	14.84	15.29	15.74	16.19	16.64	17.09	17.54	17.99	18.44	18.88	19.33
29,900-35,200 = 48.5%	16.02	16.50	16.99	17.48	17.96	18.45	18.93	19.42	19.90	20.39	20.87
35,200-45,800 = 53.4%	17.70	18.24	18.78	19.31	19.85	20.39	20.02	21.46	22.00	22.53	23.07
45,800-60,000 = 58.3%	19.78	20.38	20.98	21.58	22.18	22.78	23.38	23.98	24.58	25.18	25.78

SOURCE: Smith Barney, Harris Upham & Co.

had a taxable income of $25,000, they would be in the 44 percent bracket. New York City residents pay both state and city income taxes.

The dependence of issuers on mostly these three major investor groups—banks, casualty insurers, and individuals—has been an ongoing source of controversy in the marketplace. The buying patterns of all three groups are cyclical, dependent on the ups and downs of profits and interest rates. Some observers have called for a broadening of the market for municipal bonds by giving the issuers the option to offer taxable bonds. Such an option, it is argued, would attract a wider, more stable spectrum of investors. This issue is discussed more fully in Chapters 8 and 9.

Commercial Banks

Commercial banks are heavy buyers of municipal bonds when their loan demand is relatively soft and credit is readily available, beginning usually when the economy is slack and interest rates are low, and continuing well into the next business cycle expansion. Demand for business loans generally gathers strength late in a business cycle. As loan demand picks up steam and credit generally tightens, the banks slow their buying of municipal bonds and some liquidate portions of their holdings. This pattern has been followed fairly consistently in the post-World War II period.

Throughout the 1960s, the commercial banks sharply increased their share of municipal bond purchases. The higher level of purchases was spurred by the institution of certificates of deposit in 1961. By allowing the banks to issue these short-term demand deposits to corporations, the Federal Reserve also gave the banks more flexibility to manage their own assets and liabilities. Where banks formerly invested heavily in short-term government issues to stay liquid, they could now raise money when necessary by issuing CD's. With this freedom, the banks started to switch into short and medium-term municipal bonds for their higher after-tax returns.

In 1960, the proportion of municipal bonds to all credit market instruments held by commercial banks was only about 8 percent. By 1971, the figure had risen to over 15 percent. In addition, bank assets in total were growing very fast throughout the 1960s. The result was that the banks bought about 60 percent of new issues of municipal bonds offered during the period. (See Figure 6-3.)

FIGURE 6-3.   Share of Commercial Bank Assets Held in State and Local Government Securities, 1952-1980

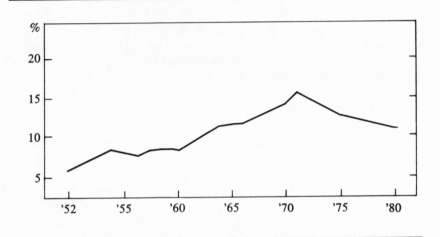

SOURCE: Federal Reserve Flow of Funds Accounts

The amount of municipal bonds as a proportion of commercial bank portfolios increased sharply during the 1960s.

That growth was not to be repeated in the 1970s. For one thing, the banks found other ways to reduce their tax liabilities. Leasing operations, through which banks could make ample use of the investment tax credit, became very popular, and foreign tax credits for many major banks were significant. In addition, early in the 1970s the profits of some banks were drained partly by real estate investment trust losses and a generally weaker economy. As a result of these factors, municipal bond holdings declined somewhat as a proportion of their total investments.

Commercial banks usually invest in municipal securities of short and medium-term maturities to assure themselves liquidity. Commercial banks also own municipal bonds to pledge as collateral for public deposits. In addition, municipal bonds can be used for collateral at the discount window of the Federal Reserve.

Casualty Insurance Companies

Besides commercial banks, casualty insurance companies are the only other financial institutions where the combination of investment objectives and high tax rates makes municipal bonds attractive in large amounts. Insurance company profits are cyclical, and the companies generally are only big buyers of tax-exempt securities when their profits are running strong. In the mid-1970s, insurance company purchases of municipal securities were particularly strong because of increases granted by state regulators. Worsening inflation, however, cut sharply into earnings as the costs of claims rose. Also, regulators generally have been slow to grant insurance companies rate increases to compensate for inflation. During the 1970s, rate increases were allowed only after significant declines in earnings. As a rule during such cycles, profits generally remain squeezed for some time, and purchases of municipal securities fall off rapidly.

Aside from the tax exemption, an important advantage of municipal bonds to casualty insurance companies is that bonds are recorded on the financial statements at cost rather than market value. According to most state laws, stocks must be recorded at market value when computing the surplus of a casualty insurer. The surplus, in turn, determines how much insurance a company is allowed to write. By holding municipal or taxable bonds and not stocks, the insurer will not be penalized by fluctuations in market prices. With municipal bonds, the company will gain the tax advantage as well. By the end of the 1970s, the proportion of casualty insurance company assets devoted to municipal bonds was about twice as high as it was in the 1950s.

Casualty insurers usually favor long-term maturities for their municipal bond portfolios. They are principally interested in producing the highest yield possible, given adequate credit quality. Long-term municipal bonds produce the highest returns. Similarly, many casualty insurers prefer revenue bonds over general obligation securities to produce higher returns on their investments. (See Figure 6-4.)

Individual Investors

Individuals buy municipal bonds from dealers, dealer banks and through bank trust departments, as well as through open-end and closed-end bond funds. Their activity in the market fluctuates widely, with the

FIGURE 6-4. Share of Property and Casualty Insurance Company Assets Held in State and Local Government Securities, 1952-1980

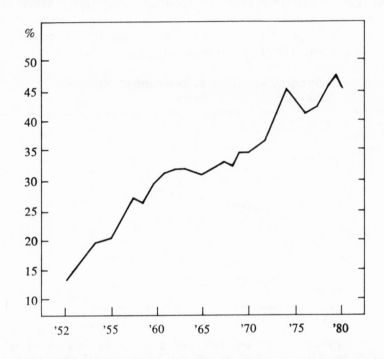

SOURCE: Federal Reserve Flow of Funds Accounts

The proportionate share of property and casualty insurance company assets held in municipal securities has more than tripled since the early 1950s.

greatest volume of purchases normally when municipal rates are near their highest levels. In 1969, to take one extreme example, interest rates were at their cyclical peak and individuals accounted for the purchase of almost 97 percent of net new municipal issues. In 1974 and 1975, municipal rates rose to unusually high levels compared to corporate rates, and individuals were again attracted to the market by high interest rates to absorb more bonds than any other single group of investors.

Individual interest in municipal bonds in the 1970s was not merely attributable to higher interest rates. Inflation pushed the entire population into higher tax brackets. With more investors in higher tax brackets, the

demand for bonds increased. Studies of the tax rates of investors who
hold municipal bonds have not been updated recently, but in the past
they have shown that municipal bond ownership is heavily concentrated
among investors in tax brackets of 50 percent and higher. While the
amount of tax-exempt income paid to the investor is static, say, 10.00
percent ($100.00 per thousand dollars), the benefit is progressive. The
progressive benefit is illustrated in Figure 6-5.

FIGURE 6-5.   Progressive Value of Tax-Exempt Income
(on a 10% Tax-Exempt Bond)

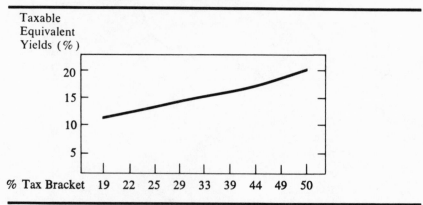

SOURCE: Public Securities Association

**For an individual investor who purchased a tax-exempt bond with a 10%
coupon initially, when he was in the 39% bracket, the taxable equivalent yield
would have to be 16.39%. The same 10% coupon would be equivalent to a
20% taxable yield when the same investor reaches the 50% bracket.**

Some observers believe that based merely on tax rates, and their
progressive nature, it would make sense for individuals to own more
municipal bonds than they actually do. But many who are eligible
because of high incomes have not accumulated the wealth to enable
substantial purchases, especially if they want to diversify their assets.
Generally, bonds now trade in $5,000 denominations. As with most other
securities, spreads on smaller trades are usually higher than for large
trades. The bond funds, both closed-end and open-end, go a long way
toward making municipal bond investments more accessible to the
general public. Their extraordinary growth since their inception has
introduced an important new element into the municipal bond demand
equation.

The Basic Principles of Investing in Bonds

One fundamental relationship in fixed-income securities pricing is that as interest rates rise, prices fall and as rates fall, prices rise. But the degree to which prices shift is affected by several important factors.

MATURITY

The longer the maturity, the wider will be the swings in prices for any change in interest rates. A bond with a coupon of 6 percent due in six months would have to sell at 95 to produce a 10 percent yield to maturity. That same 6 percent bond due in 12 years would have to sell at 72 to yield 10 percent a year to maturity. The investor obviously must wait 12 years to receive the full par amount of the bond, the full $1,000. In the first example, an extra $50 gain over 6 months is sufficient to bring the yield to maturity up to 10 percent. In the second example, a $280 discount is required to bring up the yield because this gain is spread over such a long period of time. Short-term bonds will trade closer to the $1,000 par value because the investor will receive the full amount of the principal sooner.

LEVEL OF INTEREST RATES

Generally, the higher the level of interest rates, the smaller will be price movements for any change in interest rates. If interest rates fall by two percentage points from 8 percent on high-quality ten-year bonds to 6 percent, the price of a par bond would rise by about 15 points to 115. A 6 percent ten-year bond trading at par would rise faster if interest rates fell two percentage points from that level. The price would rise to about 116½ if interest rates fell from 6 percent to 4 percent.

DISCOUNTS AND PREMIUMS

Bonds trading at a discount will swing widely in price for a given shift in interest rates. Bonds trading at a premium will shift proportionally less. Those selling at large premiums (generally above the call price) are referred to as cushion bonds. Take the case of two 20-year bonds that both yield 6.5 percent to maturity. The discount bond has a coupon of 2 percent and is selling for 50. The other carries an 8 percent coupon and sells for nearly 117. If the market were to push the yield to maturity on both bonds to 7.5 percent, the discount bond will fall by about 6½ points to 43½. The premium bond, on the other hand, will fall by 11½ points. But the percentage change in the price of the bonds is the key calculation. The price of the discount bond will have dropped by 13 percent, whereas the price of the premium bond will have dropped by only 10 percent.

Similarly, bonds with higher coupons shift in price less for a given change in interest rates than bonds with lower coupons, whether or not they are selling at a discount or premium. The lower the coupon, the greater will be the adjustment in price in order to compensate for the change in yield. Because gains earned on discount bonds are taxable, the prices of discount bonds will fall even lower than these calculations suggest.

Investor Objectives

The extraordinary range of securities in the municipal bond market allows investors to meet a wide variety of needs. Casualty insurance companies look for high yields and will usually buy long-term bonds. Fluctuations in the prices of these bonds, while wide, do not affect the companies' records for statutory purposes, as noted. Commercial banks seek more flexibility because they are likely to raise or reduce their holdings relatively quickly. Banks will therefore buy bonds in short- and medium-term maturities. Short-term maturities are generally easier to sell, and there is less risk of taking a loss because they fluctuate less in price than longer-term issues.

Individual investors can be long-term buyers, while others want a measure of liquidity. Some look for high current yields only, while others may seek capital gains over the long run. A summary of basic investor objectives follows, along with examples of how municipal bonds can meet those objectives.

HIGH CURRENT INCOME

Current yield is the simple coupon rate divided by the price paid for the bond, without regard to maturity date. A wealthy retired couple, for example, might want to live on their current investment income. They could buy a municipal bond selling at a premium. In such cases, the current yield would be higher than the yield to maturity. The premium is not deductible as a tax loss, however.

For investors more willing to take risks, but still seeking current income, there are a number of lower-rated bonds to choose from. For example, at one point in time, a New York State Municipal Assistance Corporation bond due in 2008 was priced to yield about 8.6 percent at the same time that a higher-quality Illinois bond was yielding 5.20 percent.

ADVANTAGES OVER THE LONGER TERM

Discount bonds are often appropriate for investors less interested in current income than in long-term gains. The gains earned when the bond matures are taxable. But for investors who will be in a lower tax bracket when the bonds come due, municipal bonds can serve the purpose and bring some tax-free income in the meantime.

TIMING THE MATURITY

There are so many securities available in the municipal marketplace that it is possible to tailor a bond portfolio to fit special timing needs. For parents who may have children entering college in ten years, for example, discount bonds that mature then might be appropriate. Investors can stagger maturities if they are not certain of cash needs in the future. There are a variety of one-to-three year maturities for the short-term investor. The note market, with maturities of less than one year, is suitable for investors who want maximum liquidity.

IF THE INVESTOR MOVES

In an increasingly mobile society, tax-exempt bonds have a drawback. Bonds issued in one state are often not exempt from taxes in the other states. For the itinerant investor, there is a recourse. The issues of Puerto Rico, Guam, the Virgin Islands, and Washington, D.C., are exempt from state and local taxes in all states.

SWAPS

Swapping is one of the most useful investment techniques among fixed-income investors. The most popular use of municipal bond swaps is to produce a loss for tax purposes that can be used to offset capital gains, or, to some extent, ordinary income.

Essentially, a swap is just what its name suggests. An investor sells one security and simultaneously buys another with the proceeds, usually for about the same price. In a tax swap, the investor will have a loss on the bond to be sold, probably because interest rates have risen since the security was bought. The objective is to take the tax loss to offset gains elsewhere, but without substantially changing the dollar value, risk level, yield, or maturity of the investment.

Investors must realize that they cannot have it all their own way, however. For one thing, the Internal Revenue Service requires that the issues being swapped are not "substantially identical." Otherwise, the trade is ruled a "wash sale" and the tax loss will be disallowed. Tax accountants interpret what is identical or not in different ways, and each tax swap should be carefully reviewed. A trade involving different issuers is considered a good swap for meeting IRS standards. In lieu of this, accountants generally say there must be a significant difference in coupon or maturities.

There are other costs to the trade. The dealer will earn a spread, and the perfectly exchangeable issue is not easy to find, even when it is legally allowable. Usually, investors will want to maintain quality and keep the total amount of the investment the same. They also usually want to maintain the same level of current tax-free income. Often, to satisfy all the requirements, an issue with a longer maturity is bought.

An example of a *practical* tax swap follows. At the end of 1976, an investor owned $50,000 par value of an issue that he bought at par with a 5.20 percent annual coupon rate. Interest rates had risen substantially, and the sale of the bond would produce a substantial loss. The investor decided to take the loss by selling the issue and investing the proceeds in a similar issue. His dealer worked out the following trade.

SELL

Rating	Par Amount	Coupon Rate	Date of Maturity	Current Price	Current Yield	Yield to Maturity
Baa	$50,000	5.20%	9/1/90	76¼	6.82%	8.09%

BUY

A	$50,000	5.25%	12/12/95	75	7.00%	7.80%

The proceeds from the sale of the issue were $38,125, the original purchase price was $50,000, and the resulting loss was $11,875. The cost of the purchased issue was only $37,500. Through the swap, the investor raised the current yield slightly, and improved the credit rating a notch. But something was also given up in the process. The maturity on the purchased issue was five years longer than on the former issue, and the yield to maturity was nearly 30 basis points lower. Furthermore, at maturity, the investor will incur capital gains tax.

Swaps can be used for a variety of other purposes. Investment managers will often swap in and out of securities they find more attractive than other securities. Swaps between bonds in the tax-exempt market and those in the taxable market are not uncommon. Generally, swaps are a key investment technique in implementing more sophisticated investment strategies of institutions and large investors.

Call Provisions

Most municipal securities in the high and volatile interest rate environment of the 1970s were issued with call provisions. To the investor, call provisions are a potential penalty that generally must be compensated for with higher coupon payments when the bonds are issued. Bonds are usually called when interest rates have fallen below the level prevailing when the bonds were issued. The issuer can refund the bonds and offer a new issue at the lower rates. But the investor whose bonds have been called is left with funds that can be invested only at lower rates. The opportunity to earn further capital gains on the old bonds is cut off.

Investors should be aware of the call protection remaining on any bonds purchased. Typically, bonds are not callable from five to ten years or more after they are issued, although bonds have been issued that are callable immediately. The call price is usually, but not always, at a premium to par. Often, there are a series of succeeding call dates for an issue of bonds with a declining call price for each succeeding call date. Calls are either optional or mandatory and can be for an entire issue or part of one. Bonds are generally called in reverse order of maturity. When only part of an issue is called, the bonds are usually redeemed at random by lottery. These provisions should be spelled out in the official statement and bond resolution.

As noted in Chapter 3, the yield to call will show investors what yield will be earned if the bonds are called. It is the equivalent of the yield to maturity, except that it is calculated to the first call date and price.

The yield to call, if lower than the yield to maturity, must be cited in written confirmations of orders. Bonds with little time left to the first call date will often trade at lower prices and higher yields to maturity than equivalent bonds with ample call protection, especially when interest rates are high and are expected to fall, a condition that would make a redemption likely.

One option open to investors who want to avoid a call is to buy deep discount bonds. When interest rates rise, bonds with low coupons will fall sharply in price. Such bonds are less likely to be called if interest rates fall because they are paying such a low coupon rate already. Other important considerations for municipal discount bonds are discussed below and in Chapter 8.

Sinking fund call provisions can work to the detriment of the investor in much the same way that other call provisions can. But in some situations, sinking funds can prove an advantage. For one thing, the sinking fund reduces the credit risk of the issue because monies are being set aside to pay off principal and interest. Second, sinking fund provisions usually call for the issuer to redeem bonds at the call price or to buy bonds in the open market if they are trading below the call price. The purchase of these bonds by the issuer can help support the price of the bonds in the market.

Investor Strategies

More aggressive investors, institutional and fund portfolio managers, as well as some individuals, will seek other ways to improve their performance. Some basic strategies follow.

INTEREST RATE SWINGS

Some investors try to anticipate wide swings in interest rates. If rates are thought to be going up, an investor might liquidate to the extent possible holdings in all long-term bonds, including municipal bonds. If rates are going down, investors might build up the portfolio. For practical reasons, institutional investors cannot often make radical shifts in the amount of their holdings. One alternative is to move part of a portfolio into short-term maturities in anticipation that interest rates will rise. The drop in the price of short-term securities will be less than in longer-term issues for a given rise in interest rates. Similarly, an investor might choose to go with longer-term issues if interest rates are likely to decline.

Bolder investors might invest in deep discount bonds if interest rates are expected to fall. The faster price movement in these bonds could produce substantial gains. For investors who believe that interest rates will rise, premium bonds will serve the purpose of shielding the portfolio somewhat against wide price swings.

Some investors who are particularly uncertain about the course of interest rates adopt a fence-straddling position. They can invest heavily in long-term bonds for the attractive yields. But they also might place a substantial portion of their funds in securities with very short-term maturities to give them flexibility should interest rates turn sharply in either direction. Because investors concentrate their holding at both ends of the maturity spectrum rather than in the middle, this technique has been dubbed a "barbell" strategy.

SPREADS

Investors will often invest in classes of securities whose yields are historically out of line with other securities in the market, or in anticipation of a shift in these relationships due to changing market conditions. When interest rates are very high and investors are particularly concerned about a weakening in the economy, the yields between low-rated securities and higher-rated securities often widen. Some investors will sell their more risky investments and move into the highest-rated securities. In times of easier credit and greater confidence, some investors will begin to buy the lower-rated bonds. Swapping between bonds of different quality is quite common among institutional portfolio managers. (See Figures 6-6a and 6-6b.)

Similarly, the spread between bonds with long maturities and short-term bonds also varies under different market conditions. When these spreads are out of line compared to historical relationships, investors frequently shift into the more attractive segments of the market.

Capital Gains Taxes

While municipal bond investors do not have to worry about taxes on interest income, capital gains taxes can play an important part in

FIGURE 6-6a.   Yield Spreads Between Aaa-Rated and A-Rated Municipal Securities (2-month shift➤)

FIGURE 6-6b.   Yield Spreads Between Long- and Short-Term Municipal Securities (6-month shift➤)

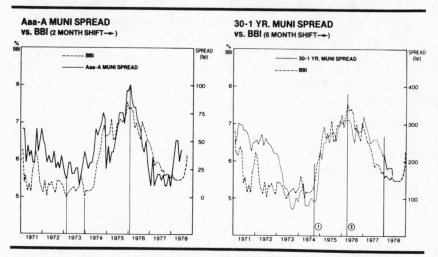

SOURCE: Bankers Trust Company

Sophisticated investors try to forecast the spreads between issues of different maturities and different quality ratings. These spreads often follow a cyclical pattern. Figure 6-6a shows how quality spreads have widened nearly coincidentally with the Bond Buyer Index. As shown in Figure 6-6b, maturity spreads are slower to respond to movements in the Bond Buyer Index.

determining the best investment strategies. In general, any profits due to a rise in price or the redemption of a bond bought at discount are taxed at the normal capital gains rate. By and large, the same capital gains tax laws that apply to other securities also apply to tax-exempt bonds because they are transactions between investors and do not involve the municipality directly.

A gain is considered long-term if the security has been held for more than one year. The holding period begins on the trade date, the day the trade occurs, rather than the settlement date. The holding period ends on the day of sale. Any security held for one year or less results in a short-term gain. Any gain realized from covering a short position is short-term for tax purposes.

All short-term gains and losses, as well as long-term gains and losses, are netted against each other to determine the total short-term gain or loss and long-term gain or loss for the year. That is, short-term gains are totaled and reduced by the total of short-term losses to determine the net short-term gain or loss. Similarly, all long-term gains and losses are added together to determine the net long-term gain or loss.

In turn, net long-term losses can be used to offset net short-term gains dollar for dollar, and net short-term losses can be used to offset net long-term gains. If net long-term losses, say, are greater than net short-term gains by $1,000, the investor reports a long-term loss of $1,000. If net short-term gains are greater by $2,000 than net long-term losses, the investor reports a short-term gain of $2,000. Similarly, net long-term capital gains might either exceed net short-term losses or fall short of the losses. In the first case, the investor would report the long-term gains. In the second, the investor would report the short-term losses. (See Appendix.)

The passage of the Economic Recovery Tax Act of 1981 changed the taxation of short and long-term capital gains. Short-term capital gains are taxed at the taxpayer's ordinary income tax rate which will be a maximum of 50 percent beginning with the 1982 calendar year. Also beginning on January 1, 1982, long-term capital gains will be taxed at a maximum of 20 percent. Short-term losses can be used to reduce ordinary income of individual and corporate taxpayers by up to $3,000 a year. Any extra losses can be carried forward to offset gains in future years. In contrast, it takes $6,000 of long-term losses to offset $3,000 of ordinary income. Excess long-term losses may also be carried forward.

Other Tax Matters

PREMIUM BONDS

When an investor holds a bond to maturity that was bought at a premium, he or she will not incur a tax loss on the difference between the purchase price and the par value. If the bonds are sold at a loss before maturity, the size of the loss will depend on how long the bonds were held because the law requires that the premium be amortized on a straight-line basis and deducted from the tax basis. The premium of $40 a bond for an issue bought at 104 and due in twenty years, for example, would be amortized at $2 a year. If the investor sold the bond at 101 in ten years, the reportable long-term loss is only $10. The $30 difference between the purchase price of 104 and the sale price of 101 must be reduced by the total amortization of the premium. At $2 a year for ten years that comes to $20.

DISCOUNT BONDS

The gain that results when an investor sells a bond bought at a discount for a profit or holds it to maturity is considered a capital gain. But, for certain bonds issued at a discount, called "original-issue discounts," the difference between the discount and the par value, under certain circumstances, is not taxable. The discount is considered part of the tax-exempt interest being earned on the bond by the investor, and must be amortized over the life of the bond. A ten-year bond with an original issue discount of $20 and sold at par in five years would still be subject to capital gains tax on $10, or half of the discount. But if redeemed at maturity, the $20 discount would be subject to no capital gains tax at all.

ACCRUED INTEREST

Municipal bonds trade plus accrued interest. The buyer, who will receive the full six months' interest if he or she is the bondholder on the interest payment date, must pay the seller the share of interest earned between the settlement date of the transaction and the last payment date. The payment of the accrued interest, which is made when the bonds are sold, is tax-exempt to the seller of the bonds.

Bond Funds

The first bond fund appeared in 1961 in the form of a unit investment trust. At that time, Congress did not yet allow tax-exempt interest income to be passed through to investors in managed mutual funds specializing in municipal bonds. But unit investment trusts could pass along tax-exempt income. Such funds buy bonds for a portfolio and usually hold them to maturity. The life of these funds is usually limited to the life of the bonds originally bought.

Investors can buy units in the funds, usually in multiples of $1,000. Although most investors intend to hold on to their investments until the bonds mature, the fund sponsors ordinarily maintain secondary markets for the units. Investors can also redeem the bonds through the funds' trustees, although the price paid for the units will have declined if interest rates rise. As the bonds in the unit trust mature, or are called, the investors who have held their units are paid back the principal value. Some fund sponsors will reinvest interest income for investors in an open-end fund set up for that purpose. There is a sales charge of 3½ percent to 5 percent for the unit investment trusts.

In 1976, Congress liberalized its pass-through ruling and allowed managed mutual funds to pass on tax-exempt income to investors and open-end funds grew rapidly. Like traditional mutual funds, the open-end funds investing in municipals can buy and sell bonds in the portfolio as often as they deem necessary. The objective is to produce a higher return by good management than would be available if bonds were simply bought and held. The prices of the bonds in the portfolio will determine the asset value of the funds, and they will shift up and down with general changes in interest rates. Sales charges run up to 8½ percent, although many are no-load funds available with no sales charge. Management fees and expenses run about 1 percent of the assets.

While closed-end funds generally invest in long-term bonds with high credit ratings, the objectives and management styles of the open-end funds vary widely. Several are devoted to short-term municipal bonds and provide investors with maximum liquidity. Others are managed very aggressively, with bonds traded frequently. Management philosophies also differ. Several bond fund managers try to time swings in interest rates and shift their portfolios between long-term and short-term maturities, as well as cash. Other managers only seek out undervalued securities.

There is a controversy over just how manageable municipal bond funds really are. Some sponsors of closed-end funds, where portfolios do not change once the trust is established, claim that interest rates are very difficult to forecast in the short run. Managers of open-end municipal bond funds, however, claim that over time they will outperform the unmanaged unit trusts.

Evaluations

Because municipal bonds are traded over-the-counter and because so many issues are traded infrequently, investors often request evaluations of their municipal holdings. Evaluations may also be necessary to satisfy legal or financial requirements for individuals and institutional investors, as well as bond funds.

The types of evaluations vary widely, but they essentially are designed to arrive at a price for each bond in a portfolio that would be received if the bond were sold that day. Most issues have not traded recently, so the evaluator tries to find similar issues that have traded. Even that, however, is usually very difficult, and can be especially time-consuming.

Many evaluations, instead, are mathematical estimates often computerized, based on a grid or matrix with three dimensions. Each dimension corresponds to one of the important variables of the bond: coupon; maturity; quality. The mathematics of the grid allows the evaluator to estimate at which price a bond with a given coupon, maturity, and quality should be currently trading.

By and large, an evaluation is only as good as the information that goes into it. For some evaluations, new market information is fed into the matrix only monthly. Others, however, will update their systems far more frequently, and in some cases daily. The accuracy of the market information is also important. An evaluator would need a good sense of how the market is trading for a full range of bonds. That information must include not only prices, but shadings in the quality that the market is assigning to different kinds of bonds. Some evaluation systems use a finely differentiated system of quality ratings, while others are very simple.

INSURANCE

Investors can buy insurance for their bond portfolios. American Municipal Bond Assurance Corp., the municipal bond insurance subsidiary of MGIC Investment Corp., will insure portfolios of a certain quality held by investors. The insurance company guarantees the payment of interest and principal on so-called investment grade issues only—bonds rated BBB by Standard & Poor's and Baa by Moody's, or better. The Municipal Bond Insurance Association, which insures bonds for issuers, will not insure investment portfolios. Dealers, however, can insure an issuer's offering on their own by taking out a policy with MBIA.

7

Credit Analysis

Few functions of the municipal bond industry received greater attention than credit analysis in the last half of the 1970s. The financial difficulties of New York City and weakened municipal finances elsewhere caught the marketplace off-guard. Investors and dealers were long accustomed to comparatively secure payment of principal and interest. There had been few serious municipal credit problems since the Depression. In the 1930s, there were nearly 5,000 recorded defaults. In the 1960s there were fewer than 300. Between 1945 and 1965, one study found that only $10 million of principal and interest was permanently lost to municipal investors. Even the Depression defaults were almost entirely corrected by 1945, and most investors were paid their debt.

The investment community is no longer as calm. Research departments for dealers as well as for institutional investors have grown markedly. Where attention once centered almost solely on a handful of debt ratios, research analysts now explore in detail the economic and administrative nature of the municipalities. They seek more information about population, wealth, and local industry. They watch for trends in employment, per capita income, and the assessed valuation of property as well as closely analyze the financial statements and seek fuller disclosure of data where necessary.

In addition, the growth in the number of complex revenue bond issues has required a broader research effort. Housing and hospital issues, for example, are financially very intricate. Airport and stadium bonds must be analyzed like any new business venture. Traditionally monopolistic enterprises such as public utilities have become larger and more complex as well. Industrial revenue bonds should be monitored closely as the security is dependent on the continued profitability of the company involved.

The two major categories of bonds are analyzed in very different ways. General obligation bonds require analysts to concentrate on the financial health of the entire community and the potential of its taxing power. The emphasis for revenue bonds is as varied as the types of revenue bonds issued. Because payment usually comes only from one source, an economic analysis of the project being financed is critical. But the legal and financial protective provisions of revenue bonds are often even more important and are given close scrutiny.

General Obligation Bonds

THE POLITICAL MOOD

One of the important lessons of the 1970s was that changes in the political mood of taxpayers can prove as important for the value of bonds as the financial ability to pay. Willingness to pay has always been an issue of municipal bond analysis. But the principle was brought home in a somewhat different way by the referendum that supported Proposition 13 in California in mid-1978 and Proposition 2½ in Massachusetts in 1980.

The new article to the California constitution cut back taxes on real property to 1 percent of full value, which is 4 percent of assessed value in the state. The limitation on tax-raising ability did not affect outstanding general obligation debt because any debt already approved was protected —that is, taxes could still be levied to pay the debt. In fact, the credit of the outstanding general obligation bonds became more secure, while new issues slowed to a trickle. But outstanding lease-rental bonds, which are paid out of general tax revenues, and tax allocation bonds, which are specifically backed by increases in property tax revenues from added property values due to district redevelopment, were severely affected.

In short, a community's action can significantly alter the credit of municipal issues that are already outstanding. While the contractual obligation of issuers to pay off general obligation debt has been strongly reinforced by the courts, an obligation cannot be met if there are no funds with which to meet it. Most revenue bonds are not affected by taxpayer limitations on property tax because they are normally paid from other sources of revenue. But there is nothing to say that electric utility users, for example, will not stage their own revolt. As a result, assessment of the current political mood of states and localities can prove to be an important part of municipal bond analysis.

Analysts also rely on other information to better understand a community's willingness to pay. The details of the constitution or the statute authorizing bonds will provide an indication of how difficult it is to raise more debt. Past action to meet budget deficits is another guide. Over the longer term, analysts prefer to see that the final maturity of bonds does not exceed the life of the project for which the proceeds are used. Future taxpayers may not regard kindly paying for an office building that is no longer being used. Also, analysts prefer an average maturity of debt that is relatively modest.

Finally, tax pledges behind general obligation bonds are often specifically limited. The limitation is usually stated as a percentage of the property that is taxable. Sometimes, however, there are stated conditions under which the limitations can be relaxed. The key question for analysts is how close the tax rate already is to that limit.

THE DEBT BURDEN

Traditional general obligation bond analysis emphasized the debt burden of the community. The objective was, and still is, to determine whether the debt of the issuer is at a manageable level compared to property values, population, income and similar data. Measures of debt burden have proved to be inadequate tools in themselves. But coupled with other information, debt burden is still an important gauge of the ability of communities to pay their debt.

The measures most commonly used are a series of debt ratios. The ratios are then compared to benchmarks based on averages throughout the country. And trends in these ratios are watched closely for signals to future improvement or deterioration. The analysis begins with the computations of the municipality's debt. A sample debt statement is shown in Figure 7-1.

The first figure of significance is total bonded debt. It is the total general obligation debt issued by the municipality, no matter what the purpose. Added to this is any unfunded debt, typically short-term notes. The sum of the two is usually called total direct debt. The next step is to deduct all items that are not actually a potential burden on the municipality's tax resources. The first deduction is for all self-supporting debt. This is generally debt issued to support a project and paid for

FIGURE 7-1.   Determining a Municipality's Debt Burden

City of Chicago Debt Statement as of January 2, 1980

Estimated Full Valuation of Taxable Property (1978) $32,927,390,148

Assessed Valuation (1978) 29.83% of Estimated Full Value   9,822,240,841

Population 1979 Estimated: 2,935,624

		Amount
Direct Debt:		
	General Obligation Bonds	246,880,000
	General Obligation Notes (1)	94,000,000
	Interim Financing Notes (1)	42,000,000
	Revenue Bonds	330,292,000
		713,172,000
	Tax Anticipation Notes Outstanding	79,900,000
Total Direct Debt		793,072,000

Less:	Self Supporting Debt		
	Water Revenue Bonds	132,650,000	
	Calumet Skyway Revenue Bonds	101,000,000	
	O'Hare Airport Revenue Bonds	96,642,000	
	TANs	79,900,000	
	Total Deductions	410,192,000	
Net Direct Debt		382,880,000	

Net Overlapping Debt (2) (3)	*Amount*	%	
Chicago PBC—City of Chicago			
Bonds	118,998,000	100.00	118,998,000
Notes (4)	28,915,000	100.00	28,915,000
Board of Education	535,952,000	100.00	535,952,000
Chicago Park District	165,136,000	100.00	165,136,000
Forest Preserve District	30,050,000	44.92	13,498,460
Metropolitan Sanitary District	373,000,000	46.03	171,691,900
Community College District #508	42,644,000	100.00	42,644,000
Cook County (5)	254,545,000	44.92	114,341,614
Total Net Overlapping Debt			1,191,176,974
Net Direct and Overlapping Debt			1,574,056,974

Per Capita Net Direct and Overlapping Debt $536.19

Percentage of Net Direct and Overlapping Debt to
Estimated Full Valuation   4.78%

(1) Represents borrowings from banks primarily for capital purposes.
(2) Includes principal amount of PBC bonds secured by leases with the following bodies: Cook County, $46,545,000; Board of Education, $141,777,000; Community College District #508, $1,318,000; Chicago Park District, $53,412,000.
(3) Includes $23,805,000 of a $100,000,000 line of credit for the PBC—the loan is distributed as follows: Chicago Park District, $7,079,000; Community College District #508, $16,376,000; Board of Education, $350,000.
(4) This $28,915,000 is also part of the $100,000,000 line of credit for the PBC.
(5) Includes $64,950,000 of a $130,000,000 line of credit.

SOURCE: Continental Illinois National Bank and Trust Company

A debt worksheet, such as the one illustrated, shows how the debt burden of a local community is computed.

out of the revenues of that project. General obligation debt, for example, is often issued to support water and sewer systems, and even airports. Although the debt may ultimately become a claim against the municipality's tax revenues, the issues are often structured to be self-supporting.

Along with deducting the self-supporting debt, any sinking funds or reserve funds established to pay off debt in the future should be deducted. The buildup in such reserves reduces the liability of the issuer. Finally, Tax Anticipation Notes and Revenue Anticipation Notes, short-term notes that will automatically be paid off out of earmarked revenues, are deducted. Bond Anticipation Notes, on the other hand, will ultimately be converted into long-term debt and are not deducted from total debt in the computation.

When these items are deducted from total direct debt, the figure left is called net direct debt. To this must be added the debt of overlapping or underlying units of government. Such units are school districts, parks, and other services in which the municipality shares, such as police or sanitation. Because the local population must also bear this debt, the related part of the debt of these units is assigned to the municipality. The amount assigned is the proportion of the municipality's assessed value to the assessed valuation of the whole unit, including the municipality. This overlapping debt is totaled and added to the net direct debt to arrive at the final figure, the overall net debt. The overlapping debt for Chicago is shown in Figure 7-2.

FIGURE 7-2. Overlapping Debt of the City of Chicago

City of Chicago Estimate of Overlapping Bonded Debt
January 2, 1979

Overlapping Bond Debt	Net Debt*	% Applicable	Amount Applicable
County of Cook	$203,012,000	50.16%	$ 101,830,819
Chicago Board of Education	580,585,000	100	580,585,000
Metropolitan Sanitary Dist.	345,850,000	51.35	177,593,975
Community College Dist. #508	33,197,000	100	33,197,000
Chicago Park District	163,515,000	100	163,515,000
County Forest Preserve Dist.	35,150,000	50.16	17,631,240
			$1,074,353,034

*Includes amounts payable under lease with Chicago Public Building Commission to retire its bonds as follows: County of Cook, $53,137,000; Chicago Board of Education, $150,055,000; Community College District #508, $1,397,000; Chicago Park District, $56,455,000.

SOURCE: Continental Illinois National Bank and Trust Company of Chicago

Direct debt alone gives a distorted picture of a municipality's debt burden. The obligations of overlapping or underlying units of government must also be taken into consideration.

With overall net debt tallied, the analyst is ready to compute a variety of ratios. The most basic measure is the ratio of overall debt to full valuation. Analysts prefer to use full market value of property rather than assessed valuation. Assessed valuation is generally a percentage of the full value of the property as set by the municipality or state. Because these percentages vary widely, a comparison of different municipalities is difficult to make. For example, assessed valuation in California is 25 percent, in Chicago it is 33⅓ percent, and in Kentucky it is 100 percent. By using full valuation, the analyst does not have to worry about variations in state formulas. A table of average ratios can be found in Figure 7-3. Many municipalities, however, have diversified their tax base, making debt to valuation a less important measure than it once was. Other debt ratios can be more meaningful.

FIGURE 7-3. Debt Ratios: Overall Debt to Full Valuation

GROUP & POPULATION RANGE

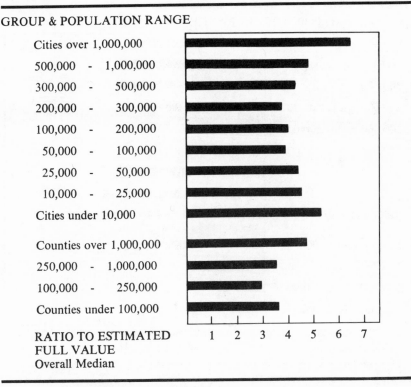

Cities over 1,000,000	
500,000 - 1,000,000	
300,000 - 500,000	
200,000 - 300,000	
100,000 - 200,000	
50,000 - 100,000	
25,000 - 50,000	
10,000 - 25,000	
Cities under 10,000	
Counties over 1,000,000	
250,000 - 1,000,000	
100,000 - 250,000	
Counties under 100,000	

RATIO TO ESTIMATED FULL VALUE
Overall Median

1 2 3 4 5 6 7

SOURCE: Moody's Investors Service

Overall debt to full valuation is one of the most basic of the credit analyst's tools for comparing the debt burden of different municipalities.

One commonly used ratio is overall debt to population. The per capita debt of a highly-rated municipality would almost certainly be less than $1,000 and normally less than $500. The wealth and income levels of the population must be considered here. Comparison of debt to personal income is also a favorite tool of analysts. Data on debt per capita are shown in Figure 7-4.

Comparing annual debt service to tax and other revenues provides a measure of an issuer's ability to pay. It is a common tool for analyzing state credits, where there usually is no property tax.

Moral obligation bonds of states present a special situation for analysis. While the full backing of the state is implied for these bonds,

FIGURE 7-4.   Average Per Capita Debt by City Size

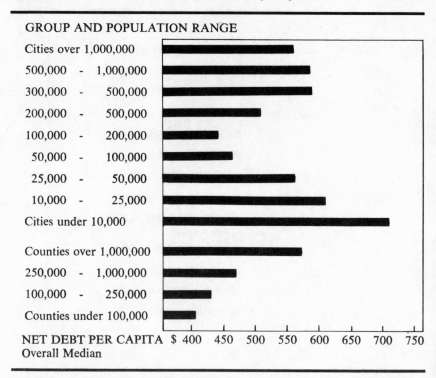

GROUP AND POPULATION RANGE

Cities over 1,000,000

500,000 - 1,000,000

300,000 - 500,000

200,000 - 500,000

100,000 - 200,000

50,000 - 100,000

25,000 - 50,000

10,000 - 25,000

Cities under 10,000

Counties over 1,000,000

250,000 - 1,000,000

100,000 - 250,000

Counties under 100,000

NET DEBT PER CAPITA $ 400   450   500   550   600   650   700   750
Overall Median

Per capita debt is an important measure of tax burden, but comparative statistics on local wealth and levels of income must also be considered when using this measure.

there is some doubt as to how readily states will rescue issues in trouble. Analysts concentrate, instead, on the degree to which these bonds are self-supporting and will not need the state's help. Standard & Poor's usually assigns a level to a moral obligation bond one notch below what they would assign to a full faith and credit bond of the same guarantor. Moody's simply ignores the moral obligation and rates the issue on its own pledged revenue support.

Vermont, Maine, and New Hampshire have set up bond banks to aid smaller municipalities in raising money. The bond bank will buy entire issues of local municipalities, financed by the floating of its own bond issue. Occasionally, the bond bank issue is backed by some kind of guarantee from the state. Proponents of bond banks argue that there are two major benefits. Pooling the issues provides some reduction of risk from diversification. And the larger issue of the bond bank is easier to market than the relatively small issues of the individual municipalities. Opponents contend the forecasted large interest cost savings have not occurred.

The best sources of financial information are the municipality's or unit's official statement and annual report as well as other financial statements it makes available on request. Moody's and Standard & Poor's provide services that summarize much of the most important data for thousands of issues.

ECONOMIC ANALYSIS

To many analysts, the state of the local economy is the most important single factor in determining a state or municipality's credit worthiness. Communities at different stages of growth may require more or less debt. A young, booming city often needs to issue more bonds than a mature or deteriorating city. A high per capita total debt or rising trends in total debt might be understandable in the first case and present a danger in the second.

Two key indications of a community's economic strength are income levels and employment statistics. Per capita income and its rate of growth is one of the first measures looked at. Some analysts also examine income per household because per capita data can often be misleading. It can be distorted by large student or prison population, for example.

Analysts caution against relying too heavily on unemployment numbers to measure the strength of employment. Patterns of unemployment can be disguised by a number of factors, including population shifts and changes in the composition of the labor force. Labor force growth is a better determinant.

By comparing the income levels and employment growth of the municipality to national averages, a sense of the community's economic standing in the country can be ascertained. Comparing these statistics to similar statistics in the neighboring regions of the municipality can help to isolate problems that might otherwise go unnoticed.

There are other readily available data that are good indications of economic health. One often-cited measure is the valuation of property per capita. The age of housing and rent levels are also good indications of local wealth.

Population can be a key indicator. A growing population is usually a sign of strength, although unusually rapid growth could lead to problems. A falling population is generally associated with deteriorating cities. Occasionally, however, a city may lose population to its suburbs, but retain its economic strength as a place of employment.

Once an overall direction of the local economy is established, scrutiny of the specific industries and companies that dominate the community's employment is important. The two principal questions are whether the main industries are healthy and growing and whether the region is diversified economically so as not to depend too heavily on any one industry, or on one sector, such as manufacturing. Expansion plans for major companies can be important. The building activity in a municipality is a way to assess these expansion plans. Overbuilding, of course, can be as dangerous as no building at all. A mix of new, sprouting companies and mature, steady companies is usually more desirable. Often, dealers or rating agencies will consult their corporate research departments for specific information on companies in a particular region being evaluated.

Diversity not only protects a community from deterioration should the major employer leave town or suffer a business setback, but it also can shield the municipality to some extent from a severe downturn during economic recessions. A good yardstick for a municipality's strength is how well it did in the last recession. Did employment recover in line with the rest of the economy? Did personal income hold up? Did the municipality run an operating deficit?

TAX REVENUES

Analysis of a locality's economics must be translated into how they affect the tax base. A strong economic structure will normally mean plenty of taxing potential. But there are several factors that should be analyzed further. Again, diversity is key. A corporation in the region may even be more dominant in terms of the proportion of taxes paid than in employment it provides.

Major sources of revenues besides property tax are also welcome. How significant are revenues from sales taxes, income tax, fees, and concessions? Because most states do not levy property taxes, a careful analysis of their various sources of income is important.

For many municipalities, Federal and state aid can comprise as much as 30 percent or more of revenues. Most analysts regard too much reliance on aid as a danger. For one thing, it is usually out of the control of the municipality, except in the case of school bonds where state aids are in addition to local taxes. For another, the amount of aid can be changed not only by legislative actions on the state and national levels, but sometimes by administrative decisions, all of which are subject to political vagaries.

Finally, once the sources of revenue are reviewed, analysts can determine what potential there is for raising tax rates. Generally, if taxes are already high, the potential for increases is less. The percentage of taxes collected in some state and local governments can run dangerously low, even when other factors look good. A poor collection rate, especially compared to rates in adjoining regions, could reflect economic shifts or simply an inefficient government.

FINANCIAL FACTORS

The emphasis on long-term factors in determining municipal financial health has certainly increased since the turbulent mid-1970s. But what has received even more emphasis has been the current financial status of the municipalities and their methods of reporting. And for good reason. What caught the marketplace off-guard in the 1970s was not so much a misinterpretation of long-term trends but a misunderstanding of the true state of local finances at that very time.

Deficits in any of the various funds municipalities use to account for their finances are a red flag that requires more investigation. In the 1970s, the size of the deficits of several major cities was far larger than what was reported. The cause of the deficit, and whether the factors are temporary and easily remedied or chronic and longer-term, must be understood. An occasional deficit is not necessarily a problem. A dip in the economy, a change in state aid, or a local corporate bankruptcy could tilt the fund into temporary deficit. A deep or ongoing deficit must be investigated further.

In relation to this, short-term financing is watched closely. Many state and local governments have adopted an active short-term financing program to provide funds when the timing of revenues and expenditures does not match. The volume of the short-term notes can reach dangerously high levels, however, which is precisely what happened in the case of New York City.

An operating deficit or surplus must be analyzed in light of the municipality's past operations. The surplus or deficit in the final balance is the sum of past surpluses and deficits, and a surplus there may more than compensate for an operating deficit in any given year. Balance sheets must also be examined. A healthy level of working capital and highly liquid current assets are beneficial. Reserves for such items as uncollected taxes and payables should be adequate.

What has compounded the problem of interpreting a municipality's current health is variations in accounting methods. The true extent of the operating deficit or surplus can be difficult to discern. The ability to switch from cash to accrual accounting or back again can mask problems in a current operating period. There is also the occasional practice of commingling funds. Revenues in a bond fund have been transferred to the general fund to make up a deficit.

Close analysis of the budget is another valuable tool. Has the municipality stayed within the budget in the past? What specific items account for the cost overruns or excesses? Is the next year's budget reliable? Some localities have adopted procedures for carefully allotting funds which must be examined.

OFF-THE-FINANCIAL-STATEMENT CONSIDERATIONS

Pension liabilities—The extent of pension fund liabilities for municipalities has drawn widespread concern. For one thing, it has often been difficult to obtain reliable information on the amount of such liabilities, although reporting has improved in recent years. Second, a great proportion of the pension liabilities are unfunded. Analysts generally want to know how pension obligations will affect expenditures over the years. If there are heavy unfunded liabilities, will the state or local government be obliged to increase outlays substantially? If funded, have the actuarial assumptions about inflation and investment returns on the funds been realistic? Could the funding have been set too low? Concerns have also been raised over the level of leasehold obligations and accrued vacation time, neither of which is customarily accounted for on government financial statements.

Depreciation—One of the debates over government accounting methods concerns depreciation (see Chapter 3). Fixed assets of state and local governments are usually recorded separately on the financial statements. Some governments do not record them at all. State and local governments do not depreciate their general fixed assets either, with the exception of those recorded in the enterprise and several other funds. In lieu of a financial account to check on, analysts will try to assess whether spending on maintenance is adequate, and whether capital improvements have been sufficient.

OTHER FACTORS

The opinion of bond counsel should not be taken as perfunctory. The reliability of counsel is critical. The role of bond counsel is discussed in greater detail in Chapter 2.

The independent audit is becoming more common among larger issuers of municipal debt. The National Council on Governmental Accounting (see Chapter 3) recommends that an independent audit of financial statements be undertaken annually. To the analyst, the independent audit helps assure the accuracy of the financial data being presented and that it is consistent with prior financial statements. Because the audit is undertaken in accordance with the NCGA's generally accepted accounting standards, the uniformity and consistency of accounting methods can be relied on. Audits supervised by state officials (most states require some kind of audit) or made to assure compliance with a government program will not necessarily address the same areas as an audit by an independent accountant using NCGA principles.

Finally, many analysts try to assess the general capability and responsibility of a state or local government's fiscal officers. More and more, analysts have come to place emphasis on how well a city or state is managed, how carefully programs are documented, and how diligently and imaginatively the future programs of the municipality are planned. Political structure can be particularly important. For example, a strong mayor system will often be able to control finances better than a weak system. When rating an issuer's credit, the more judgmental factors, however subjective, are playing an increasingly significant role.

Revenue Bonds

The analysis of revenue bonds is quite different from that of general obligation bonds. Virtually every revenue bond project is different, and an economic analysis of the demand for services, cost and operating efficiency, and competition is imperative to every analysis.

Most revenue bonds are traditionally protected by a number of legal and financial agreements that can often be more important to bondholders than the project itself. The first step in any analysis is close examination of the provisions of the bond resolution. The provisions are contained in the issue's official statement.

The Resolution

FLOW OF FUNDS

The resolution sets forth the order in which funds generated by the project will be allocated to various purposes. The funds go to pay for operations, debt service, and to establish reserves. Different kinds of bonds will require different flows of funds. But, generally, all funds will first be recorded in the Revenue Fund. The flow of funds that follows is typical of many revenue bonds. Any investment of reserves must meet the Treasury Department's arbitrage regulations. Arbitrage certificates are to be signed by a local official as part of a procedure to help assure that the requirements of the regulations will be met.

Operations and maintenance—Through the operation and maintenance fund passes the money necessary to meet the ongoing expenses of the project. Revenues will be placed into the fund monthly to meet budgeted expenses. Normally, one-twelfth of the annual budget will be shifted from the reserve fund to the operation and maintenance fund each month. From there, expenditures will be made to cover expenses. Occasionally, enough money is placed in the fund to cover budgeted expenses as well as a reserve.

Debt service—Funds are set aside monthly that will equal over the year the amount necessary to meet annual debt service. Within the fund are often separate accounts for principal and interest. Sometimes separate bond redemption funds or accounts are set up. There may also be a note repayment fund or account, and a sinking fund account.

Debt service reserve fund—After annual debt service is assured, funds are apportioned to the debt service reserve fund. These funds are tapped should the debt service fund itself be insufficient to meet annual payments. The reserve fund is usually set at an additional year's debt service, although it may equal only average annual payments rather than the maximum annual payments. This fund can be initially set up out of bond proceeds or built up over time.

Reserve maintenance fund—Allocations are made to this fund to meet unanticipated maintenance problems, usually at the recommendation of the consultants in charge.

Renewal and replacement fund—The fund is established to replace equipment and make repairs over the life of the project. A set payment is made into this fund according to the project's budget for such replacements. When more construction is planned, a construction fund is normally set up for expansion or new projects.

Surplus monies—Most resolutions will carefully itemize where the balance of revenues will be directed should they exceed what is required for all funds. The monies are sometimes used to redeem bonds or reduce tax payments. Many municipalities take surplus funds from revenue projects for use in their own general fund. The resolution also specifies what kinds of securities can be bought with excess funds.

Analysts assess all these funds to be sure they are sufficient to meet the projects' requirements. Occasionally, one or two funds may be set unrealistically low. Ample reserve funds will improve the issue's credit. In Figure 7-5, the flow of funds accounts of a typical revenue bond issue is set forth.

COVENANTS

A sensible flow of funds and ample reserves are not the only assurances investors seek. For user-charge bonds, a rate covenant is important. The issuer pledges that rates will be set sufficiently high to meet operation and maintenance expenses, renewal and replacement expenses, and debt service. Another form of rate covenant requires that rates be set to provide a safety margin of revenues above debt service after operation and maintenance expenses are met.

Additional covenants might include a provision for insurance of the project, requirements for a periodic review by a consulting engineer, that

FIGURE 7-5. Flow of Funds Account for a Typical Revenue Bond Issue

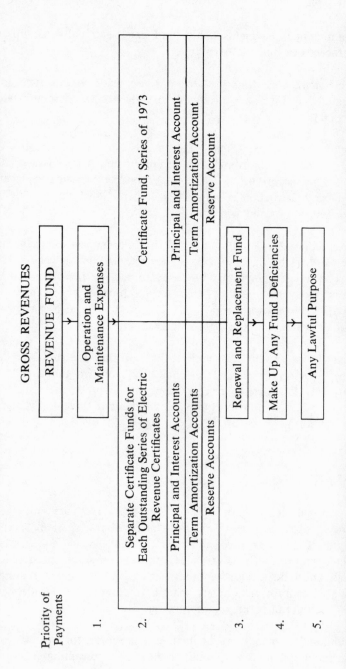

The flow of funds is the order in which the revenues generated by the project financed from the proceeds of the revenue bond issue will be allocated to various purposes.

no free services shall be offered to municipalities or other customers, that separate books will be kept to record the accounts of the project. Other covenants analysts look for are provisions for independent audits and prohibition against sale of the project or facilities until the bonds are paid off.

CLAIMS ON REVENUES

The priority of bonds as to claims on revenues is important. Bonds are usually backed by a first lien on net revenues. Most analysts note that, in practicality, operations and maintenance will have first claim on revenues if a project is in trouble. After all, bonds cannot be paid off if the project is no longer in operation. Bonds with second or third liens are rated significantly weaker. In fact, there may be debt obligations that have priority even over first-lien bonds—for example, a power supply contract is usually treated as an operating expense. Bond reserve funds for higher-priority bonds in the flow of funds also have a priority over first lien bonds.

ADDITIONAL BONDS

Once the claim on revenues has been established, a very important covenant written into most revenue bond resolutions involves provisions for additional bonds. If the issuer can offer bonds at a later time that have a parity or prior claim on revenues, the bondholder may be placed in a riskier position. Most issuers will provide one of two types of protective bond clauses. The less common one stipulates that any additional bonds will be junior and subordinate to the current bonds, except those that may be necessary for the completion of the project. This is called a closed-end provision, the drawback being that subordinated bonds will be more difficult to market.

An open-end provision allows for bonds of equivalent lien on earnings to be issued, subject to certain requirements. Generally, the limitation is that the earnings coverage of debt service including that for the new bonds not fall below a set minimum—for example, 125 percent. Earnings of the project can be defined in several ways to meet this test, however. Some define the earnings to be covered as the most recent fiscal year's earnings or the average of earnings over the preceding 24 months. The latter is the most conservative of the methods commonly used. Another method is to base the test on future estimates of earnings. This usually requires reports by reliable consultants.

ECONOMIC ANALYSIS

Most revenue bonds are supported by projects that must be analyzed just like any business venture. The factors that affect the various kinds of revenue projects will differ markedly. Basically, however, the issuer should provide a great deal of the data to investors through preliminary official statements, feasibility and other engineering studies, capital improvement programs, bond resolutions, and various reports.

Some types of projects require more scrutiny than others. By and large, water, sewer, and electric utility bonds are backed by monopolistic enterprises and are quite secure. By contrast, housing and hospital bonds usually require much more research.

Even utility bonds, however, can require some care. A comparison of rates to those in other communities in the region gives a sense of whether the charges being considered are unreasonable. Another question to be answered is whether the utility can raise rates freely without interference by the municipality or other government organization. Also, is the customer base diversified and not dependent on one major user? Is the service area growing? Are incomes of residents high and rising? Many of the same considerations that apply to analysis of the financial health of the whole municipality also apply to revenue bonds.

Within a given rating category, the market perceives housing and hospital bonds as generally riskier ventures. Financial and legal considerations are often paramount. But the demand for the service as well as the ability of customers to pay are key aspects of such analyses. Some of the most important factors affecting the credit of different kinds of revenue bonds are outlined below.

Electric utility bonds—The strength of the underlying economy is a key factor in determining the demand for electricity. The cost of the service should be in line as well. Analysts prefer to see that sources of power generation are diversified between different types of fuels. The power supply itself must be adequate to support the area's growth, and any future capital outlays should be considered. On the other hand, too low a usage rate can become a burden as well.

Water system bonds—The supply of water is generally the most important issue, but the water must meet Federal environmental standards as well, which may require special and expensive treatment. The economic base of the area being served is important in determining demand.

Toll road bonds—Once the potential traffic is estimated, the major question for future success is just how elastic is the demand. If toll rates rise, will traffic fall off a great deal? A mix of different types of users helps, especially heavy usage by commercial vehicles. Competing roadways should also be considered. Bridge and tunnel authority bonds should be examined for the same factors. Often, the bond resolution will have a provision that calls for limiting the construction of potentially competitive projects. Economic trends in the location being serviced should also be analyzed.

Industrial revenue and pollution control bonds—These credits are as good as the corporations behind them. They are backed by leases to those corporations and are usually analyzed as unsecured debt of the corporation. Often, however, the bonds are guaranteed by a corporate subsidiary and not by the parent company. In the more secure issues the investor has a first mortgage on the property involved.

Airport bonds—Generally, a feasibility study is a must in analyzing the prospects for an airport. The potential traffic through the airport is the main consideration. Is it an airport for a single, major city? Are there competing airports? Could it become a hub airport? Some airports are backed by leases to the participating airlines and should be analyzed much like industrial revenue bonds. Sometimes, however, those contracts are based on airline traffic.

Hospital bonds—Among the most complex of issues, here too a feasibility study is generally necessary. The location, level, and quality of services are important. A teaching hospital will normally have a good flow of well-trained physicians. Third-party payments by insurance companies, Medicare, and Medicaid can make up the bulk of a hospital's revenues, and analysts prefer independent insurance company payments to government payments. Care should be taken that a "certificate of need" is secured on the financing involved.

FIGURE 7-6.   Major Uses of Revenue Bonds in 1980

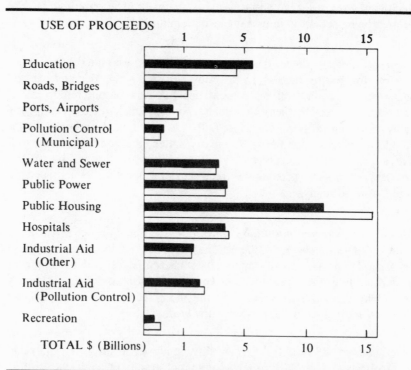

Education and public housing were the two uses to which municipalities put the largest share of the funds raised through revenue bond financing in the late 1970s.

Housing bonds—These issues have accounted for an increasing proportion of the market. Multifamily projects are generally undertaken by state housing finance agencies. The projects are typically supported by federal subsidies. The key analytical variables include the occupancy rate and the ability of the occupants to pay. Proper construction of the project as well as the quality of ongoing management are also important. Reserves for maintenance, for example, should be adequate.

Single-family bonds are issued by both state agencies and local governmental entities. The governmental unit may purchase a portfolio of mortgages. The levels of reserves and insurance coverage are key considerations. Debt reserve funds must be adequate, and most of the mortgages are usually insured independently or through the government.

There is also sometimes pooled insurance to cover part of the mortgage portfolio. The demand for mortgages in the area served is an important point to be assessed. A lack of demand can mean that the costs of the issue will not be covered. Similarly, the ability of the lending agency or institutions making the mortgages should be assessed.

FINANCIAL FACTORS

Financial ratio analysis is a useful way to assess the viability of a revenue project. The most frequently used measure of a project's well-being is the coverage ratio—the ratio of revenues, less operation and maintenance expenses, depreciation and local taxes, to debt services. The pertinent information is found in the issuer's operating statement. Besides operation and maintenance expenses, depreciation and local taxes are deducted from revenues to determine coverage.

Analysts also emphasize that projecting future debt service coverage is important. Debt service coverage may be adequate when bonds are issued, but if additional bonds are planned, or revenues fall off, that coverage could drop sharply. Analysis of the efficiency of current facilities and the potential need for new facilities plays a role here.

8

Understanding Municipal Bond Interest Rates

To the underwriter or trader in municipal bonds, pricing securities is an everyday affair. But underlying the short-term shifts in securities prices and interest rates are longer-run factors that will have a far greater impact on the course of most interest rate shifts over time. The basic principles that determine interest rates in general will also determine the level of municipal rates. Generally, municipal bond rates rise and fall with interest rate levels of other fixed-income securities. A nearly thirty-year comparison of the Bond Buyer Index to rates on Federal securities demonstrates clearly the close relationship between markets for the two securities. (See Figure 8-1.)

In the short run, however, municipal interest rates can go their own way. Municipal rates are particularly affected by the cyclical buying habits of the principal investors. The tax exemption, as discussed in Chapter 6, limits the market to those who can best take advantage of it: commercial banks, insurance companies, and high-income individuals.

Municipal rates are also permanently lower than rates on other securities of equivalent maturity and risk because of the tax exemption. In 1980, long-term municipal rates averaged approximately 65 percent of rates on equivalent corporate securities. But they have fluctuated more widely over time. Before the Sixteenth Amendment established the income tax, municipal securities traded at about the same rate as corporate securities. Within a few years, the gap between the two widened. At the end of World War II, rates on municipal bonds were as low as

135

FIGURE 8-1.   Interest Rate Trends in the Municipal and U.S. Government Securities Markets, 1950-1980

PERCENT

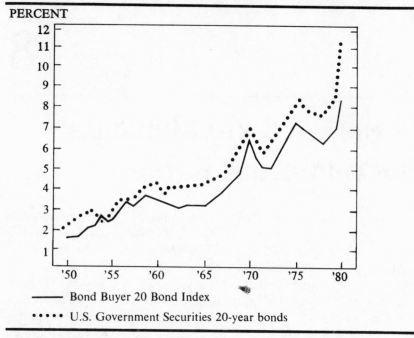

——— Bond Buyer 20 Bond Index

•••• U.S. Government Securities 20-year bonds

SOURCE: Salomon Brothers

Rates on municipal securities generally rise and fall with changes in other interest rates, although the extent and timing of those shifts can vary.

41 percent of corporate rates. The gap slowly began to narrow. Short-term notes, typically bought by large institutions taxed at corporate rates, have in recent years consistently traded at less than 50 percent of comparable corporate rates.

Determinants of the Overall Level of Interest Rates

THE BUSINESS CYCLE

One well-established observation of most economists is that, as economic activity picks up, interest rates will rise. Borrowing demands will increase across the board. Financial institutions and capital markets will compete with each other for a limited supply of funds. The banks will raise the rates they are willing to pay and raise the interest rates to borrowers as well. To attract capital to the money and bond markets, rates will have to rise further.

This process has been borne out in business cycle after business cycle. Interest rates peak at about the same time that the rate of real economic growth (adjusted for inflation) begins to decline. In inflationary periods, interest rates have generally peaked a little later in the cycle. Therefore, efforts to forecast the business cycle play an important part in interest rate forecasting.

THE FEDERAL RESERVE

The nation's central bank is one of the most powerful forces in the economy. It has considerable influence over key interest rates, as well as over the amount of reserves in the banking system that support the creation of money through bank deposits. To many economists, the growth of the money supply is the most important variable in determining the growth of aggregate spending. Others claim that fiscal policy—the primary tools being tax expenditure policies of the Federal government— is more influential. This latter economic camp also believes that the level of nominal interest rates is very important.

The Federal Reserve has several methods by which it can influence interest rates and the money supply. It sets the discount rate, the rate at which banks that are members of the Federal Reserve system can borrow directly from the Fed. It also establishes reserve requirements for its members. Banks must keep a set portion of every deposit or loan on hand as a reserve. The most flexible method of control for the Fed, and the most frequently used, is through the policy directions of its Open Market Committee. Through guidelines established by the Committee, the Fed buys and sells U.S. government securities in order either to add or withdraw reserves from the banking system. This not only alters the total amount of reserves outstanding, but also has a direct effect on the interest rates of those kinds of securities the Federal Reserve is buying or selling.

In recent years, the Fed has tried to maintain control over both money supply and interest rates. The group of economists, known as the monetarists, claims that the Fed should by and large not attempt to control interest rates but rather concentrate on controlling the money supply. Other economists hold that the level of interest rates is more important than the money supply. However, by trying to control both, some argue, the Fed is unable to control either.

Whatever the theory behind its moves, the Fed has a great influence on interest rates in the short run. When the money supply is growing too quickly or the Fed wants rates to move higher, it will direct its open-market operation to sell government securities. The added supply of securities should drive prices down and yields up. In the meantime, the Fed is draining bank reserves from the system in payment for the securities it is selling. That can reduce the money supply. Should the Fed want rates to fall, or want to boost the money supply, it will usually buy government securities.

An entire industry of Fed watchers has grown up in recent years. These economists try to anticipate the Fed's activities, and to explain the reasoning behind what moves the Fed does make. In the late 1970s, the securities markets became so sensitive to Fed policy that most interest rates would rise or fall somewhat whenever the Fed took action. Often, the market would rise or fall on the announcement of the weekly change in the money supply. If the money supply rose, interest rates rose in anticipation that the Fed would withdraw funds from the market and push rates up. An unexpected drop in the money supply would send rates lower in anticipation that the Fed would buy securities.

INFLATION

Many economists believe that inflation expectations are built into interest rates. The basic theory is that there is a real rate of interest that would prevail if prices were stable. Even if there were no inflation, lenders would demand compensation for giving up purchasing power now. Borrowers are willing to pay for the credit because they believe they can use the money productively. History suggests that the real rate of interest for long-term corporate borrowing in the United States has been approximately 3 percent. For short-term securities, the real rate has been much lower.

When prices rise, lenders demand a higher rate to compensate for their lost purchasing power. Borrowers, on the other hand, are willing to bear higher rates because they will be paying back the loan in the future with money that has lost value. If investors expect inflation to stay at 6 percent for the life of a bond, for example, they would demand an additional 6 percent of interest. That 6 percent, plus the real rate of interest, would approximate the long-term interest rate, according to this view.

Because future inflation cannot be known with certainty, the degree to which inflation is built into interest rates reflects investors' and borrowers' long-run expectations of inflation. Even short-term interest rates respond to these expectations. For whatever reasons, most economists do agree that, as inflation rises, so will interest rates. A clear indication of the direction of inflation is one of the most important factors in forecasting the level of interest rates.

THE NATION'S FLOW OF FUNDS

Interest rates are essentially the prices that will equalize the supply and demand for credit throughout the economy. If there is a great demand for credit, interest rates—the price of credit—will rise (assuming constant supply) to make it more costly to borrow as well as to attract prospective lenders. If demand for credit falls, the opposite result occurs.

Changes in the supply of credit will affect interest rates in the opposite way. More funds available to buy securities will push rates down. Many economists at brokerage firms and banks closely analyze the nation's capital flows to forecast interest rates. The object is to project the major demands for borrowing, on one hand, and to project the major sources of the supply of lending on the other. The projections, of course, are closely related to forecasts of the business cycle in general.

The Federal Reserve publishes an invaluable series of accounts to facilitate such an analysis. It is called the Flow of Funds, and traces just how money flows through the entire economy. With this tool, economists attempt to forecast the various components of the supply and demand for credit. Unusually heavy needs by municipalities, for example, or the Federal government, can be assessed in this way. Heavy demand from these borrowers may be offset by lighter borrowing needs for corporations. On the supply side, the economists can get a better notion of just how much strain will be placed on different kinds of financial institutions, as well as on the direct money and capital markets themselves. Any great increase for the major institutions would suggest a tightening in availability of credit and higher interest rates.

In 1979, total credit supplied came to $415 billion, more than twice as much money as was raised in 1974, when the economy was in a recession. The amount of credit supplied by thrift institutions was two and a half times what it was in 1974, rising from about $26 billion to $67 billion. Commercial banks more than doubled the amount of funds they supplied. The big increase in demand for funds was for mortgages, which nearly tripled to $118.5 billion. The volume of new issues of tax-exempt notes and bonds was 50 percent higher than in 1974.

FIGURE 8-2. The Supply and Demand for Credit

1. Summary of Supply and Demand for Credit ($ Billions)

	1974	1975	1976	1977	1978	1979	1980	Amt. Out. 31 Dec. 79
			Annual Net Increases in Amounts Outstanding					
Net Demand								
Privately Held Mortgages	42.2	42.0	70.4	109.0	116.5	118.5	100.7	1,102.9
Corporate & Foreign Bonds	29.1	39.1	39.1	37.4	33.5	32.8	42.7	475.6
Subtotal Long-Term Private	71.3	81.1	109.5	146.4	150.0	151.3	143.4	1,578.5
Short-Term Business Borrowing	50.4	−16.0	9.8	47.0	78.5	112.9	81.5	577.3
Short-Term Other Borrowing	16.3	14.4	40.7	49.6	66.0	62.3	43.9	486.6
Subtotal Short-Term Private	66.7	−1.6	50.5	96.6	144.5	175.2	125.4	1,063.9
Privately Held Federal Debt	28.4	82.6	71.8	73.3	83.8	66.9	96.5	760.0
Tax-Exempt Notes and Bonds	14.5	16.3	17.1	31.1	32.9	22.0	27.0	328.0
Subtotal Government Debt	42.9	98.9	88.9	104.4	116.7	88.9	123.5	1,088.0
Total Net Demand for Credit	180.9	178.4	248.9	347.4	411.2	415.4	392.3	3,730.4
Net Supply[1]								
Thrift Institutions	25.8	53.7	70.0	81.8	80.2	66.7	58.8	738.1
Insurance, Pensions, Endowments	29.0	40.9	53.1	67.3	70.2	75.1	81.4	690.6
Investment Companies	1.7	3.7	4.6	6.7	8.3	23.2	20.7	57.4
Other Nonbank Finance	3.9	4.3	8.7	17.6	15.9	25.6	19.5	185.6
Subtotal Nonbank Finance	60.4	94.0	136.4	173.4	174.6	190.6	180.4	1,671.7
Commercial Banks[2]	52.6	29.9	59.6	83.5	107.0	124.3	100.0	1,091.9
Business Corporations	8.8	11.6	7.7	4.9	4.5	10.3	12.2	121.4
State & Local Government	1.1	2.4	4.9	11.3	14.7	5.2	3.0	72.5

Foreign[3]	18.5	7.1	19.6	44.1	57.4	21.7	34.6	249.0
Subtotal	141.4	145.0	228.2	317.2	358.2	352.1	330.2	3,206.5
Residual (mostly household direct)	39.5	33.4	20.7	30.2	53.0	63.3	62.1	523.9
Total Net Supply of Credit	180.9	178.4	248.9	347.4	411.2	415.4	392.3	3,730.4
Percentage Growth in Outstandings								
Total Credit	9.3	8.4	10.8	13.6	14.2	12.5	10.5	
Government	7.8	16.8	12.9	13.4	13.2	8.9	11.4	
Household	7.0	6.3	11.6	14.9	14.9	12.8	9.1	
Corporate	14.2	3.6	7.4	11.9	14.1	16.1	11.8	
Long-Term	8.2	8.6	10.7	12.9	11.7	10.6	9.1	
Short-Term	12.5	-0.3	8.5	14.9	19.4	19.7	11.8	
Held by Nonbank Finance	7.2	10.4	13.7	15.3	13.4	12.9	10.8	
Commercial Banks	8.3	4.3	8.3	10.7	12.4	12.8	9.2	
Foreign	23.0	7.2	18.5	35.1	33.8	9.5	13.9	
Household Direct	13.9	10.3	5.8	8.0	13.0	13.7	11.9	
Economic Correlations								
Growth in Real GNP	-1.4	-1.3	5.9	5.3	4.4	2.7	-1.5	
Nominal GNP	8.1	8.2	11.3	11.6	12.0	11.8	9.5	

SOURCE: Salomon Brothers

Interest rates are essentially the prices that will equalize the supply and demand for credit, and a detailed look at the credit flows is an important tool for forecasting rates.

[1]Excludes funds for equities, cash and miscellaneous demands not tabulated above.
[2]Includes loans transferred to books of nonoperating holding and other bank-related companies.
[3]Includes US branches of foreign banks.

Term Structure of Interest Rates

Why do fixed-income securities of about the same risk but different maturities trade at different yields? A pictorial description of the relationship among bonds of different maturities, which is known as the term structure of interest rates, is the yield curve. A yield curve for government securities is given in Figure 8-3. The vertical axis shows the yield, and the horizontal axis marks the years to maturity. Following the curve across to the vertical axis, one can see that a security maturing in one year yielded 7.90 at the time. A twenty-year bond yielded 8.47. The points that make up the curve are the actual yields for securities with the stated number of years left to maturity.

FIGURE 8-3. The Yield Curve

The Term Structure of Interest Rates for U.S. Government Securities, June, 1978

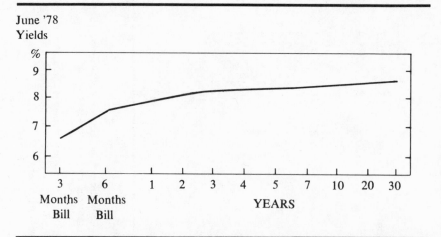

SOURCE: Salomon Brothers

The yield curve, which plots the interest rates of securities with equivalent risk but different maturities, typically slopes upward; the longer the maturity, the higher the rate.

The yield curve in Figure 8-3 is typical because it is positively, or upwardly, sloped. The yield curve is usually more positively sloped when the economy is at its cyclical low in a recession. Short-term rates are particularly low at that point. When the economy is at its peak growth rate and starting to strain its resources, the yield curve is usually inverted. A sample curve, taken in 1979, shows how short-term rates were higher than long-term rates as money tightened at the height of economic growth. Short-term rates tend to fluctuate much more widely over an interest rate cycle than do long-term rates. (See Figure 8-4.)

There are several related theories to explain the shape of the yield curve. A summary of the most important ones follows.

EXPECTATIONS

A theory that most economists adhere to in one form or another is that investors' and borrowers' expectations of future changes in interest rates are the primary determinant of the term structure of rates. The theory in its pure form assumes that investors seek to maximize their returns, regardless of the maturity of the fixed-income securities they buy. Borrowers are considered indifferent to the maturity of their debt as well. As a result, the long-term interest rate becomes the average of the current short-term rate and the expected level of future short-term rates. As expectations of short-term rate levels change, so do current levels of both short-term and long-term rates.

When investors expect future short-term rates to rise more than the general market does, for example, some will buy short-term securities and sell longer-term securities. They reason that they will earn a better return by rolling over their short-term investments than by keeping their funds in long-term securities. Their action forces current short-term yields down as they buy, and longer-term yields up as they sell. Borrowers will borrow longer-term now in anticipation that short-term rates will be higher in the future. The increase in the supply of long-term debt also drives rates up. The result is that these lenders and borrowers cause the yield curve to slope upward more steeply, reflecting expectations that interest rates will indeed be higher in the future.

When investors and borrowers expect short-term rates to decline more than the general market does, the opposite result occurs. Investors sell their short-term securities and buy longer-term because they believe the return will be greater. Borrowers defer their longer-term debt issues and instead borrow short-term. The combined action causes short-term rates to rise and longer-term rates to fall. The yield curve turns downward.

LIQUIDITY PREFERENCE

One major problem with this theory, say many economists, is that longer-term securities fluctuate more in price than short-term securities

FIGURE 8-4.   Inverted Yield Curve

The Term Structure of Interest Rates for U.S. Treasury Securities, September, 1979

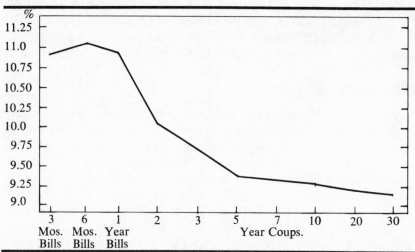

SOURCE: Salomon Brothers

Occasionally, the yield curve is inverted with short-term rates higher than longer-term rates. This occurs when the economy is near its peak rate of growth and the availability of credit tightens significantly.

when interest rates shift. If yields rise, the price of a long-term security will fall much faster than that of a short-term security. The investor who wants to sell may have to take a significant loss.

These economists claim that, to make up for risk of interest rate fluctuations, yields for longer-term securities must be higher than the expectation theory described above implies. The longer the maturity, the greater this premium. If investors and lenders all believed that future short-term rates will equal current short-term rates, the expectations theory predicts that the yield curve will be flat. Those who believe there must be a risk premium argue that the curve will still be sloped upward.

SEGMENTED MARKETS

At the other end of the theoretical spectrum are those economists who believe that interest rates are primarily a function of the supply and demand for bonds at different maturities. These economists argue that most investors and borrowers will not be willing to shift into different maturities simply because yields change. They will tend to buy and sell within a range of maturities for a variety of reasons. Banks, for example, tend to lend in shorter-term ranges. The supply and demand for funds at those maturities would then be the principal determinant of rates.

At one point, for example, there may be a very light investment demand for securities with maturities between five and ten years. Or very few borrowers may be coming to market with issues that mature in longer than twenty years. In each of these so-called segmented markets, rates will be set independently of what is going on in other maturities, claim proponents of this theory. The greater the supply of bonds compared to demand in a maturity, the higher will be rates, regardless of rates at other maturities. The lesser the supply, the lower will be rates. The shape of the yield curve, then, will depend mostly on the supply and demand for securities at different maturities.

Municipal Bond Rates

Economists generally take all the above factors into consideration when making forecasts of the overall level and term structure of interest rates. The municipal bond market, however, has several special features that must be emphasized. By far the most important of these is the unusual nature of the demand for municipal securities. As discussed in Chapter 6, the advantages of the tax exemption generally limit municipal bond purchases to commercial banks, property and casualty insurance companies, and high-income individuals.

SUPPLY AND DEMAND

Because of the specialized market for tax-exempt securities, highly cyclical demand factors are probably more important in determining municipal rates than in determining the rates of most other types of fixed-income securities. The particular characteristics of the three major buyers of municipal bonds make for a cyclical pattern of demand.

Commercial banks typically are heavy buyers of municipal bonds when most interest rates are falling and in the earlier stages of an economic upturn. At that time, loan demand is not yet strong, credit is readily available, and banks have plenty of funds to invest. As rates on other securities rise faster, credit tightens and loan demand picks up, funds will become tighter for the banks. They will begin to divert funds into their highly profitable loans, and may start liquidating some municipal bond holdings.

As the heaviest buyers of municipal bonds, the banks' purchasing patterns are very important. They own about 40 percent of all bonds outstanding. Moreover, they prefer short- and medium-term bonds because they are more liquid, and better match the maturities of their liabilities.

The casualty insurance companies also purchase municipal securities in a cyclical pattern. The level of their purchases depends mostly on their profits. Profits are strongest when inflation is stable or after regulatory commissions grant rate increases. As inflation rises, the value of claims against the insurance company also rises, which squeezes profits. Inflation is worst often at the top of, or for several months after, a downturn in the business cycle. The insurance companies will then typically start to reduce their purchases. Casualty insurance companies, which own about 20 percent of all municipal securities outstanding, will usually make their heaviest purchases later in the business cycle than do commercial banks. They tend to buy long-term bonds and lower quality bonds than banks do. The insurance companies are major purchasers of revenue bonds.

Individual investors generally are the last in the business cycle to start buying heavily. Their major inducement is high rates. As rates move up, individuals jump aboard and can be taking down the majority of municipal bonds when rates are at their very highest. The open-end municipal bond funds may throw this pattern off somewhat. Sold in much the way equity mutual funds are sold, they tend to attract a lot of money when the net asset value of the fund is rising—that is, when interest rates are falling and bond prices are rising. Their greatest purchasing power may come when bond prices are near their peaks, and yields are at cyclical lows.

The flow of funds during the economic upturn of the mid-to-late 1970s can be seen in Figure 8-5. Commercial bank purchases were largest in 1977, falling off somewhat in 1978. In 1978, casualty insurance companies were raising the level of their purchases. Their investments had been heavier than usual throughout the period because in the mid-1970s they won rate increases from regulatory agencies that helped keep profits high. Individual investors pushed up their purchases in 1977 and 1978 above earlier levels. Purchases of open-end bond funds were largest in 1980.

FIGURE 8-5.   Net Changes in Purchases of State and Local Government Securities by Major Investing Groups, 1970-1980

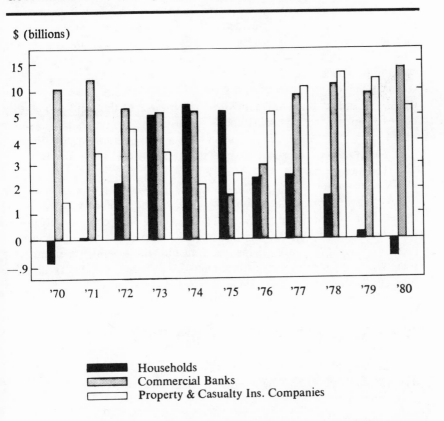

SOURCE: Federal Reserve Flow of Funds Accounts

The pattern of purchases of municipal securities by the three important investment groups varies sharply. Commercial banks have been the heaviest buyers when rates are declining or just beginning to rise, while individuals usually have bought heaviest when rates are near their peaks.

CAPITAL GAINS TAX EFFECTS

One other factor that affects municipal rates differently than it does rates on other securities is the capital gains tax. While interest payments are tax-exempt, capital gains earned upon selling bonds are taxed at the regular capital gains rates except in the case of original issue discounts as discussed in chapter 6. The investor in a discount municipal bond, for example, will receive his or her interest payments tax-free. But when it comes time to cash in the bonds, capital gains tax will be due on the difference between the par value and the purchase price of the bonds. Accordingly, discount bonds usually trade at higher yields to maturity and lower prices to make up for the capital gains tax, than will bonds for which most of the yield to maturity comes from the tax-exempt coupon. Accordingly, a high-coupon bond at about par will usually trade at a somewhat lower yield to maturity than an equivalent bond of the same maturity that has a low coupon and is priced at a discount.

For corporate and government bonds, just the opposite occurs. The typically lower rates on capital gains make the already-taxable bonds more attractive because capital gains are taxed at a considerably lower rate than interest income. Discount corporate bonds trade at somewhat higher prices and lower yields as a result. In general, when interest rates rise, municipal bonds selling at a discount will fall faster in price than equivalent corporate or Federal government bonds.

The Differences in Municipal Rates

The special characteristics of the municipal bond market result in three distinct differences between municipal and other rates.

VOLATILITY

In percentage terms, municipal rates are generally more volatile than other rates. A casual observation of Figure 8-1 reveals how much wider the yield fluctuations are for the Bond Buyer Index than for U.S. government securities. Several more sophisticated statistical studies have corroborated this.

The causes for the volatility have been discussed. The cyclical pattern of demand for municipal securities adds volatility to the market. The wider price swings of discount bonds to compensate for the capital gains tax does as well. Corporate and government bonds actually fluctuate less than they would otherwise because of the lower tax rates on long-term capital gains than on interest income.

UPWARD-SLOPING YIELD CURVES

The yield curve for municipal bonds is almost always upward-sloping, even when interest rates are near cyclical peaks. A sample yield curve from 1979 is shown in Figure 8-6. By contrast, the yield curve for Treasury securities, shown in Figure 8-4, sloped downward, reflecting the market's expectation that future rates would fall.

The composition of demand mostly accounts for this upward-sloping curve. Banks generally dominate the market for municipal securities. Because they confine most of their purchases to short-term and medium-term securities, rates in these areas will stay comparatively low as credit begins to tighten. To repeat, short-term rates usually trade at only 50 percent or so of equivalent corporate securities, while long-term rates trade at about 65 percent or 70 percent of comparable corporate securities. During periods of cyclically high interest rates, short-term municipal securities will continue to trade at about 50 percent of the yield on equivalent taxable securities. Long-term municipal securities, however, will trade at somewhat higher relative rates. Even if the market expects rates in general to fall (the corporate yield curve would be downward-sloping), the municipal yield curve would slope upward.

LAGS

Finally, upturns and downturns in municipal rates tended to lag the turning points in other rates in the 1970s. Banks have been steady buyers of municipal bonds when the economy is slow and early in an upturn in the business cycle. When their purchases fall off, casualty companies have taken up much of the slack because inflation has not yet peaked, profits are still strong, and municipal rates are at attractively high levels. This one-two punch of sorts keeps a lid on rates for a while.

Then individual investors have usually picked up the load. They will generally be induced into the market as municipal rates rise relative to taxable rates. One study shows that the Bond Buyer Index in the 1970s lagged turns in the Federal funds rate by about 15 months. It lagged turns in the discount rate by about 10 months. And the lag between the Bond Buyer Index and 20-year government bond was about a year. Figure 8-7 shows how closely the Bond Buyer Index of 20 bonds and the 20-year U.S. government bonds tracked when the rates for the government bonds are shifted forward 12 months.

FIGURE 8-6.   Yield Curve for Municipal Securities*

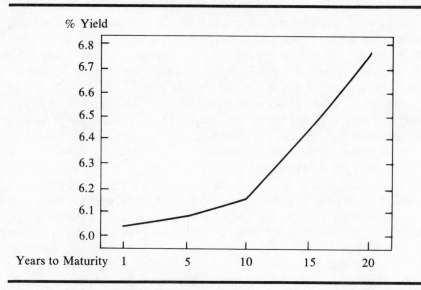

SOURCE: PSA Municipal Securities Data Base

*Moody's Aa-rated general obligation securities, average new-issue reoffering yields, October, 1979.

Because banks are the largest buyers of short-term municipal securities, these securities generally have an upward-sloping yield curve, even though yield curves for other securities might slope downward. Banks buy short-term and have a marginal tax bracket of close to 50%. This keeps the tax-exempt/taxable ratio for short-term paper close to 50%. The long-term ratio will fall as rates rise.

FIGURE 8-7.   The Bond Buyer Index vs. Yields of 20-Year U.S. Government Bonds (12-month shift➤), 1971-1978

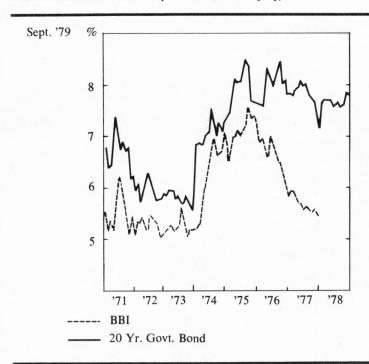

Sept. '79

------ BBI

—— 20 Yr. Govt. Bond

SOURCE: Bankers Trust Company

In the 1970s, the cyclical buying pattern of municipal investors has resulted in a lag between changes in government and corporate rates and municipal rates. Changes in the Bond Buyer Index have lagged changes in rates on 20-year Treasury bonds by about one year.

9

Regulation

Until the late 1960s, the municipal marketplace had been relatively free of Federal restrictions, and until the 1970s was not subject to extensive regulation by any Federal agency. The Internal Revenue Code had expressly exempted interest on municipal bonds from tax since 1913, when the Sixteenth Amendment was passed. The Depression of the 1930s resulted in the enactment of the Securities Acts of 1933 and 1934, but Congress expressly exempted municipal securities and issuers from most of the requirements of these Acts imposed upon corporate securities transactions. While the Securities and Exchange Commission was established as the Federal body with regulatory authority over the issuance and trading of corporate securities, the issuers of, and brokers and dealers in, municipal securities continued to be free from comprehensive SEC regulations. Municipal market participants, however, have been subject to the coverage of the antifraud provisions (Section 17 of the 1933 Act and Section 10 [b] of the 1934 Act) and rules promulgated thereunder by the SEC.

By the late 1960s the movement toward greater Federal involvement in the municipal securities market was beginning to grow. This Federal regulation has emanated from two distinct sources: first, restrictions under the Internal Revenue Code on the eligibility of the tax exemption for certain types of securities issued by state and local government units; second, the development of a comprehensive regulatory scheme under the securities laws by the Municipal Securities Rulemaking Board covering the activities of brokers and dealers of municipal securities.

In the area of restrictions on the tax exemption for municipal obligations, the Revenue and Expenditure Control Act of 1968 defined and limited the issuance of industrial development bonds. In the following year, Congress enacted the arbitrage bond statute as part of the Tax Reform Act of 1969. Within the statutory framework provided by these two laws, the Treasury and the Internal Revenue Service have promulgated detailed regulatory restrictions regarding the issuance of tax-exempt obligations.

The Municipal Securities Rulemaking Board was established under the Securities Acts Amendments of 1975. This direct Federal regulation came as a result of fraud actions brought by the SEC against some municipal securities professionals and a perception by Congress that greater investor protection was required. The composition and operation of the Rulemaking Board, the development of its rules, and its relationship to other regulatory authorities are discussed more fully later in this chapter.

An important issue during Congressional consideration of the Securities Acts Amendments of 1975 was whether the legislation would extend regulation to issuers of municipal securities, thus raising the possibility of the promulgation by the SEC of disclosure requirements for municipal bond issues. During consideration of the bill on the Senate floor, an amendment was adopted that made clear that regulation was not to be extended to issuer disclosure practices. At that time Senator Harrison A. Williams, Jr., of New Jersey, who had sponsored the original bill leading up to the regulation of dealers, stated:

> . . . the bill is not intended to tamper in any way with the prerogatives of State and local governments in their sale of securities. The amendment thus states that the Municipal Securities Rulemaking Board may not impose on issuers, directly or indirectly, disclosure requirements. Surely there can be no argument with that result.

Even though the adoption of Federal disclosure requirements for issuers was expressly precluded under the 1975 amendments, the question has remained of concern to some members of Congress, and the financial difficulties of some cities and the SEC investigation of securities offerings by New York City have kept alive interest in this subject. Several bills have been introduced in recent years to provide for Federal regulatory involvement in the disclosure and accounting practices of state and local governments.

The Basis of the Tax Exemption

A large, but by no means unanimous, body of legal opinion adheres to the view that there is a constitutional basis for the tax exemption. The basis is the constitutional doctrine of "reciprocal immunity." The doctrine holds that the states are immune from Federal interference in their affairs, just as the Federal government is immune from state interference. Since the landmark Supreme Court case of *McCulloch v. Maryland* in 1819, it has been established that the Federal government is immune from state interference, including interference by taxation. The converse immunity of the states from Federal interference has also been established by judicial precedent. The doctrine was applied by the Supreme Court in 1895 to interest on municipal bonds in *Pollock v. Farmers' Loan and Trust Company.*

At issue in the *Pollock* case was whether an income tax law enacted by Congress in 1874, which levied a tax on income including that derived from interest on municipal bonds, was constitutionally valid. Article I, Section 2 of the Constitution (until the adoption of the Sixteenth Amendment) required that direct taxes among the states be apportioned according to population, and Article I, Section 8 of the Constitution required that indirect taxes, such as duties and imports, be uniform throughout the United States.

In the *Pollock* case the Supreme Court decided that the new law was unconstitutional because taxes levied were not apportioned according to population. But the justices also held—unanimously—that interest on state and local securities clearly was not subject to Federal tax. One Justice wrote: "The tax upon income of municipal bonds falls obviously within the other category, of an indirect tax upon something which Congress has no right to tax at all, and hence is invalid. Here is a question, not of the method of taxation, but of the power to subject the property to taxation in any form."

Another Justice wrote the following: "These bonds and securities are as important to the performance of the duties of the State as like bonds and securities of the United States are important to the performance of their duties, and are as exempt from the taxation of the United States as the former are exempt from the taxation of the States."

Some legal authorities believe that when the Sixteenth Amendment became effective in 1913, the reciprocal immunity doctrine no longer applied and the Federal government was free to tax municipal interest. That Amendment reads as follows:

The Congress shall have the power to lay and collect taxes on incomes, from whatever source derived, without apportionment among the several states, and without regard to any census or enumeration.

Proponents of the view that the Federal government is able to tax the interest earned on municipal bonds cite specifically the phrase "from whatever source derived" in support of their conclusion.

Opponents of this view vociferously argue that such was not the intention of the Sixteenth Amendment. Rather, they claim, the Amendment was written to do away specifically with the need to levy taxes uniformly or according to population as the constitutional provisions originally mandated. In 1920, the Supreme Court upheld this point of view in *Evans v. Gore.* The decision stated: ". . . the genesis and words of the Amendment unite in showing that it does not extend the taxing power to new or excepted subjects, but merely removes all occasion otherwise existing for an apportionment among the states of taxes laid on income, whether derived from one source or another. And we have so held in other cases." Thus, it appears that the phrase "from whatever source derived" was intended to make clear that both direct and indirect taxes were covered by the Amendment.

By and large, decisions of the Supreme Court throughout the century have upheld this view. For example, a decision of the Court in 1938 read, "a tax on the interest payable on state and municipal bonds has been held to be invalid as a tax bearing directly upon the exercise of the borrowing power of the Government."

A look at Congressional debate when the Sixteenth Amendment was being considered also demonstrates how deeply the immunity theory was held. Governor Hughes of New York expressed concern to the New York Legislature during the ratification process that the words "from whatever source derived" could permit the taxation of interest on municipal bonds. Several Senators claimed that there was no reason to fear this result. Senator Borah responded to the concern of the Governor of New York in the Senate as follows: "To construe the proposed Amendment so as to enable us to tax the instrumentalities of the state would do violence to the rules laid down by the Supreme Court for a hundred years, wrench the whole Constitution from its harmonious proportions and destroy the object and purpose for which the whole instrument was framed."

Attempts to levy a tax on municipal interest continued after 1913, although without success. A revenue act was drafted during World War I that contained a provision to tax the interest on municipal bonds, but the provision was finally left out of the bill. Congress apparently recognized that a constitutional amendment might have been needed to tax such interest. The House of Representatives passed a proposed constitutional amendment in 1923 to authorize the taxation of income derived from future issues of municipal bonds, but the proposal failed to pass the Senate. Other Federal attempts to tax municipal bonds were made in the 1940s without success. One involved an IRS suit to require the Port of New York Authority to pay Federal taxes. The U.S. Court of Appeals for the Second Circuit ruled against it.

During consideration of the Revenue Revision of 1942 the Treasury Department strongly urged the imposition of a tax upon the interest of all state and municipal bond issues, including both present issues and future issues. This proposal was rejected by the House Committee on Ways and Means but was accepted by the Senate Finance Committee with respect to future issues. After extensive debate on the floor of the Senate, this proposal was defeated and stricken from the bill.

The most recent attempt to tax municipal interest occurred in 1969, when, as part of the Tax Reform Act, the House-passed bill included interest earned on municipal bonds within its minimum-tax provisions. The Senate did not accept the measure. Since that time, the approach has been to whittle away at certain specific uses of tax-exempt financing or to attempt to provide either the issuers of municipal bonds or the bondholders the option of including the interest derived from municipal bonds in taxable income, with the differential between tax-exempt and taxable interest rates to be made up by Federal subsidy.

The Administration's 1978 Tax Program included a proposal that would have given state and local governments the option of issuing taxable securities and to receive an interest subsidy from the Federal government. Although this taxable bond option (TBO) was advocated as a means of assisting weaker municipal credits to raise capital and to improve tax equity, it was opposed by state and local officials, chiefly because of the Federal intervention they feared would accompany the interest subsidies. Congress rejected the TBO but the Senate Finance Committee did approve an amendment to the 1978 tax legislation that would have given the option of including municipal bond interest in income to the bondholder, with a Federal tax credit to be given to the taxpayer making the election. This so-called bondholder taxable option (BTO) was later withdrawn during Senate floor debate. It was introduced by its sponsor, Senator John Danforth of Missouri, as a separate bill in 1979, but no legislative action has been taken on the proposal.

Thus, although the tax exemption has been subject to numerous assaults at the Federal level, it has prevailed. Supreme Court decisions following the principle established in *Pollock v. Farmers' Loan & Trust Company* and the continued deference of Congress to the constitutional doctrine of reciprocal immunity have kept alive the arguments for the constitutional basis of the tax exemption. Indeed, proponents of this position believe that the Supreme Court's decision in 1976, in the important case of *National League of Cities v. Usery,* adds a great deal of support to the notion that state and local governmental matters are free from Federal interference. In that case, the Court invalidated the 1974 amendments to the Federal Fair Labor Standards Act, which had extended Federal minimum wage and maximum hour provisions to almost all state and municipal employees. Although the Court acknowledged that the regulations at issue were "undoubtedly within the scope of the Commerce Clause," it found that wage and hour determinations with respect to functions which state and local governments are created to provide were matters "essential to separate and independent existence" of the states and, consequently, beyond the reach of Congressional power. Thus, although *National League of Cities* did not deal directly with the issue of the tax exemption, it demonstrated a view by a recent Supreme Court that state and local governmental affairs should be free from excessive Federal interference.

The Current Statutory Exemption

The exemption from taxation of state and local interest payments to bondholders was written into the Federal income tax law in 1913, when the Sixteenth Amendment was adopted. The Internal Revenue Code of 1954 now governs Federal taxation, and Section 103 contains the Federal statutory limitations on the exemption from taxation. Section 103(a)(1) of the Code generally excludes from gross income interest on "the obligations of a State, a Territory, or a possession of the United States, or any political subdivision of any of the foregoing, or of the District of Columbia."

The current statutory exemption, however, is not as easily determined in all cases as a reading of Section 103(a) of the Code might lead one to conclude. In 1968 Congress enacted the industrial development bond statute (currently Section 103(b) of the Code) as part of the Revenue and Expenditure Control Act of 1968. That statute substantially restricted the uses for which tax-exempt industrial development bonds could be issued. Under current law interest on industrial development bonds is taxable, with certain exceptions. The statutory exceptions include: residential real property for family units; sports facilities; convention or trade show facilities; airports, docks, wharves, mass commuting facilities, parking facilities, or storage or training facilities directly related to any of the foregoing; sewage or solid waste disposal facilities for the local furnishing of electric energy or gas; air or water pollution control facilities; facilities for the furnishing of water under certain conditions; development of industrial parks; and "small issue" industrial development bonds that are subject to dollar amount limitations. In addition to the restrictions contained in the law, the Treasury has adopted detailed regulations under Section 103(b) that further define the types of facilities that can be financed with tax-exempt bonds and that limit the degree of private credit behind the bonds.

The Tax Reform Act of 1969 eliminated the statutory exemption for arbitrage bonds—bond issues in which the proceeds are used to acquire other securities that produce a higher yield than the interest cost on the tax-exempt bond issue. Congress at that time was concerned that some state and local governments were misusing the tax exemption by investing the funds from bond issues in higher-yielding Federal or other obligations, the interest on which was not taxable in their hands. As under the industrial development bond statute, the Treasury Department has promulgated extensive regulations detailing the uses of municipal bond proceeds for investment purposes. Indeed, under Treasury regulations finalized in 1979, arbitrage bonds were broadly disqualified from tax exemption. The regulations read that any "artifice or device" used to circumvent the regulations would result in the bonds being considered arbitrage bonds. Issuers must now invest bond proceeds at rates that return a minimal yield above the interest costs in order to retain the tax exemption.

There are several major exceptions to the restrictions, which are spelled out in the highly intricate regulations. Bonds issued to finance construction projects are generally free of investment yield restrictions if 85 percent of the proceeds are spent on the project within three years. There must also be a "substantial" obligation to begin the project within six months, usually evidenced by expenditures of 2½ percent of the costs, or $100,000, and the project must proceed with due diligence. A second exception is for "reasonably required reserve funds," such as a debt service reserve fund. Such a fund cannot constitute more than 15 percent of the face amount of the issue, known as the "minor portion." The final exception is for interim investment funds, basically debt service funds. These funds must be used up within 13 months.

While these are the essential exceptions, there are others, and the rules regarding the ones mentioned are more detailed than can be set forth in this book. Bond counsel is a virtual requirement in determining the arbitrage status of issues. For any issue of $2.5 million or less, an unqualified legal opinion that the bonds are not arbitrage bonds is usually all the assurance that bondholders need. Still, arbitrage certificates signed by the issuer are generally issued to accompany offerings and they are reviewed by counsel. The Treasury regulations specifically permit the use of such certificates to establish the most reasonable expectations for the future use of the funds to be sure that they will meet the requirements of the rules.

In some circumstances, an issuer might want to refund an issue before the call date in order to issue new bonds. This might typically occur when interest rates have fallen sharply. Sometimes an issuer wants to be relieved from restrictions in the bond resolutions as well. The issuers can issue new bonds at the lower rates and use the proceeds to defease the prior issue. The proceeds are pledged to pay off the old issue and are invested in fixed-income securities of low risk, such as Federal securities, that will yield a return equal to the yield on the refunding issue.

In the mid-1970s, issuers structured such financings even when interest rates had not fallen. The rate earned on the proceeds could be used to cover not only the yield on the old issue, but also other costs of issuance, including the underwriters' spread. Any temporary decline in the amount of annual debt service between the prior and new issues, typically put into a sinking fund, could also be invested at higher rates on taxable securities. But the new arbitrage regulations specifically disallowed both practices, and advance refundings have slowed to a trickle. In periods of falling rates, however, they may become more prevalent again.

The Treasury and IRS have engaged in other efforts to restrict and control municipal financial practices in recent years. In early 1976, the Treasury proposed new regulations setting forth requirements under which public authorities and other governmental entities could qualify to issue bonds "on behalf of" a state or political subdivision. The rancor of municipal market participants over the proposed regulations has thus far prevented them from being issued in final form. In late 1977, the Treasury announced regulations with retroactive effectiveness that restricted the advance refunding of industrial development bonds.

A means of obtaining judicial relief from the regulatory actions of

Treasury and IRS has been legislatively established. In the Revenue Act of 1978, Congress devised a special procedure under Code Section 103, which permits municipal issuers to seek declaratory judgments in Federal courts challenging IRS rulings or Treasury regulations relating to bond issues.

In April, 1979, the battle shifted from the regulatory to the legislative arena when legislation was introduced by the Chairman of the House Committee on Ways and Means and other members of the House of Representatives to limit drastically the use of tax-exempt bond issues by state and local governments to provide financing of single-family homes. Legislation in this area was finally adopted in December 1980, when the Congress passed the Mortgage Subsidy Bond Tax Act of 1980. This legislation imposes substantial limits on tax-exempt mortgage revenue bonds and has had the effect of reducing the volume in this segment of the market significantly.

The Municipal Securities Rulemaking Board

The Municipal Securities Rulemaking Board (MSRB) was created as an independent, self-regulatory organization charged with primary rulemaking authority for the municipal securities industry. The MSRB's regulatory authority covers dealers, dealer banks, and brokers in municipal securities, but, as was discussed earlier, its jurisdiction does not extend to the issuers of municipal securities. All market participants subject to MSRB jurisdiction are required to register with the SEC. In 1979, more than 1,700 dealers, dealer banks, and brokers were so registered. As a self-regulatory organization, the MSRB is not financed by the Federal government, but solely by the municipal securities industry. Its operations are supported by fees and assessments paid by firms and bank dealers engaged in the municipal securities business, including an initial fee for all municipal securities brokers and municipal securities dealers registered with the SEC and an assessment based on the volume of new issue underwriting in which a firm or bank dealer participates.

The Regulatory Structure

When the 1975 Securities Act Amendments were being considered by Congress, the MSRB was designed as the rulemaking body for the municipal market with a view toward the unique nature of the municipal market and its participants—banks, securities firms engaged in a general securities business, and sole municipal firms. The MSRB is composed of 15 members. Five members of the Board represent broker-dealers, and another five represent bank dealers. The remaining five, the "public representatives" on the Board, cannot be associated with either group. One of the five public representatives must represent investors, and another must represent issuers of municipal securities.

The initial 15 members of the Board were appointed by the SEC in September, 1975. Subsequently, new Board members have been nominated and elected by the MSRB under a procedure that allows for recommendations of individuals for nomination by the industry and interested members of the public. While not involved directly in the election procedures, the SEC must, pursuant to statute, approve the selection of public members of the Board.

The Securities Act Amendments grant the MSRB general rule-making authority over municipal market participants and specify several areas of mandatory rulemaking in which the Board is required "as a minimum" to propose and adopt rules. These enumerated areas include standards of professional qualification; rules of fair practice; record keeping; the minimum scope and frequency of periodic compliance examinations; the form and content of quotations relating to municipal securities; sales of new issue municipal securities to related portfolios during the underwriting period; the definition of a "separately identifiable department or division of a bank" for purposes of SEC registration and enforcement of Board rules; the internal operation and administration of the Board; and assessments.

The MSRB's rulemaking procedures involve several steps. Generally, the Board will issue rule proposals in exposure draft form, providing a public comment period of up to 60 days. Upon adoption by the MSRB in final form, rule proposals are filed with the SEC and the Federal bank regulatory agencies. Each proposed rule is published in the Federal Register and is subject to a public comment period of up to 35 days from the date of the publication. The Board's rules are ordinarily subject to approval by the SEC prior to becoming effective. Exceptions are rules relating solely to administration of the MSRB and assessments that are effective upon filing, but may be rescinded by the SEC within 60 days thereafter.

Even though the MSRB is charged with primary rulemaking re-sponsibility over municipal market professionals, the SEC retains ultimate regulatory authority. As will be discussed later, the SEC and the MSRB have been in disagreement as to whether a rule is appropriate regarding the disclosure of markups and markdowns in "riskless" principal transactions by municipal dealers.

In recognition of the existing regulatory structure for banks and securities firms, the MSRB does not have inspection or enforcement authority. Instead, under the Securities Acts Amendments, the SEC, the National Association of Securities Dealers, Inc., for its members, and the three Federal bank regulatory agencies are charged with inspection responsibility and enforcement of the Board's rules, which have the force of law under the legislation.

THE RULES

The Board completed writing most of its rules within its first two years. Subsequently, it has been concerned with amendments, and interpretation of the existing rules. These rules are separated into three major categories. The first two are administrative and definitional. The third group, the general rules, are the substantive rules of the Board. The details of the most important of these rules have already been discussed. A brief summary of the major rules is given below, but the descriptions are at best simplifications meant only as a guide. According to the Board's Rule G-29, all dealers must keep a copy of the rules on the premises. The Public Securities Association has published a pamphlet called "A Guide to Writing a Compliance Manual for MSRB Rules."

ADMINISTRATIVE RULES

These rules, A-1 through A-15, cover such areas as membership, powers, and meetings of the Board. The rules outline the rulemaking procedures and set fees for registered dealers, as well as assessments of underwriters. As of 1979, each dealer paid a minimum annual fee of $100. Assessments were based on the volume of underwriting a dealer had done. The assessment rate was 3¢ for every $1,000 par value of bonds underwritten in 1979.

DEFINITIONAL RULES

These are a short set of rules that provide formal definitions of certain key but legally ambiguous terms (D-1 through D-11). A bank dealer, a customer, and a discretionary account, for example, are carefully defined.

GENERAL RULES

As of 1979 there were 35 general rules proposed, the key ones having already been outlined in earlier chapters. G-1 defines just what operations qualify under the rules as an independent dealer department of a bank. Professional qualifications are generally covered in Rules G-2 through G-7. G-3 is the most far-reaching, classifying employees and establishing qualifying examinations. Chapter 3 discusses this rule at some length.

The principal record-keeping rule is G-8, the details of which have been summarized in Chapters 4 and 5. Rule G-9 specifies how long records must be preserved and G-10 designates people to be responsible for record keeping.

Syndicate practices have been among the more controversial areas of coverage. Rule G-11 lists the MSRB's requirements. They are summarized in Chapter 4. The MSRB has set uniform practices for clearing, processing, and settling transactions under Rule G-12. Again, the key points are summarized in Chapters 4 and 5. Rule G-15 contains requirements for written confirmations to customers, the most important of which are outlined in Chapter 5.

Rule G-13 requires that all quotations by dealers must represent actual bids and offers. That is, the dealer must be prepared to make the trade at that yield or price at the time the quotation is made. Dealers can, however, give mere indications of yields or prices when requested as long as it is made clear that these indications are not actual quotations. G-16 states that every municipal securities dealer will be examined for compliance to the rules by the assigned enforcement agency at least once every two years.

Most of the remaining rules—G-17 through G-35—are known as the fair practice rules. These are designed, in the words of the act, "to prevent fraudulent and manipulative acts and practices, to promote just and equitable principles of trade, to foster cooperation with persons engaged in regulating, clearing, settling, processing information with respect to, and facilitating transactions in municipal securities, to remove impediments to and perfect the mechanism of a free and open market in municipal securities and, in general, to protect investors and the public interest."

The first of these rules (G-17) states simply: "In the conduct of its municipal securities business, each broker, dealer and municipal securities dealer shall deal fairly with all persons and shall not engage in any deceptive, dishonest or unfair practice."

The most controversial of the fair practice rules has been G-23, which places certain disclosure requirements on financial advisors who act as underwriters for the same issue. Details are in Chapter 4. This rule was finally approved by the SEC in 1980. Some of the other fair practice rules involve gifts, relationships between underwriters and issuers, dissemination of official statements or similar disclosure documents, advertising, the fairness of prices and commissions, and the improper use of assets.

The final rule, G-35, establishes arbitration procedures for dealers and customers who have disputes or claims involving municipal securities transactions. The MSRB has written an arbitration code that creates an arbitration committee of seven, three members of which are from the MSRB. The Code covers the initiation of proceedings by a dealer or customer, the conduct of hearings, and awards. There is a simplified procedure established for claims of $2,500 and less.

Current Regulatory Issues

"RISKLESS" PRINCIPAL

The Securities and Exchange Commission has challenged the MSRB's decision *not* to write a rule regarding the disclosure of markups and markdowns in connection with so-called "riskless" principal transactions by municipal market professionals. These "riskless" transactions are those in which a dealer has lined up a buyer or seller of municipal securities and then engages in a search of the marketplace to purchase or sell the securities. In the view of the SEC a riskless principal transaction is essentially the same as an agency transaction in equity securities. Since brokerage commissions are required to be disclosed on customer confirmations in the equity securities market, in 1977 the SEC suggested that the MSRB consider developing such a disclosure rule for riskless principal transactions in municipal securities.

In February, 1978, the MSRB advised the SEC that, on the basis of its analysis, it believed that "the imposition of a requirement to disclose remuneration in principal transactions in municipal securities is unnecessary and inappropriate." Although the SEC never formally responded to the MSRB's letter, in September, 1978, the Commission issued a release proposing to amend one of its own rules under an antifraud provision of the Securities Exchange Act of 1934 to require disclosure of remuneration in riskless principal transactions. The MSRB and the municipal securities industry have opposed this effort by the SEC. To date, no further action has been taken by the Commission with respect to the proposal.

DISCLOSURE

There is no more sensitive issue among state and local governments than the possibility of Federal requirements for disclosure of information to accompany new issues of bonds. Corporate prospectuses are required by law to be reviewed by the SEC prior to new issues of bonds and stocks. Although municipal issuers were exempted from the Securities Act of 1933, the question of whether the Federal government should be involved in developing disclosure and accounting standards for municipal issuers is still being debated. Several bills relating to the subject have been introduced in Congress since 1975. Senator Williams, who has sponsored three disclosure-related bills, stated that his proposed Municipal Securities Full Disclosure Act of 1977 would require "preparation on a uniform basis of annual reports and distribution documents and delineating and clarifying the responsibilities of issuers, underwriters, and others involved in issuing or distributing municipal securities."

Opponents generally argue that disclosure requirements are unnecessary, would be very costly, and may indeed be unconstitutional. They also argue that in response to the problems of the mid-1970s most major municipalities have made their disclosure information more accurate, cogent and pertinent, as well as comprehensive. In an effort to head off Federally mandated disclosure requirements, the Municipal Finance Officers Association (MFOA), through the combined efforts of issuers, underwriters, and bond lawyers, has developed and is revising on an ongoing basis, "Disclosure Guidelines for State and Local Governments."

Lawyers point out, however, that simply because there are no Federal disclosure requirements does not mean issuers would not be liable for insufficient disclosure under the Federal antifraud laws. Underwriters and bond counsel might also be liable. Antifraud provisions are found in both Securities Acts, as well as in Rule 10b-5 of the SEC. Because the risk of investment in municipal bonds has characteristically been low, little attention has been paid to the antifraud provisions. But their implicit demand that all material information be disclosed in an offering, virtually all lawyers agree, is directly applicable to municipal issuers as well as to other market participants.

THE ANTIFRAUD PROVISIONS

Potential action taken under the antifraud provisions of the securities laws by the Federal government and individuals clearly has important implications for issuers, dealers, and bond lawyers. Reassessment of responsibility under the antifraud laws became a growing concern in the latter half of the 1970s. As discussed earlier, the basic questions for issuers involved better disclosure, and careful accounting and auditing procedures. It is generally believed that state and local employees could also be found personally liable for improper disclosure as the antifraud provisions are clarified over the years.

One of the most controversial issues still unclarified is the extent of investigatory responsibility of underwriters and bond counsel. The SEC investigation of New York City finances made the following highly sensitive conclusion about bond counsel:

> Until late February, 1975, bond counsel passing upon New York City did little if any independent investigation and relied almost exclusively on City officials. . . . However, when put on notice of circumstances that called into question matters basic to issuance of their opinion, bond counsel should have conducted an additional investigation. And bond counsel with knowledge of information material to investors should have taken all reasonable steps to satisfy themselves that those material facts were disclosed to the public.

The SEC did not take action against bond counsel or underwriters in the New York City case. Still, bond counsel and underwriters have become more vigilant. Many bond attorneys will now closely review the official statement to be sure all material facts are presented. Some firms will dig deeper. It seems clear that all participants in an offering of municipal securities have developed a greater awareness of the need to disclose all material facts relating to the issue.

Appendix:
Mathematical Calculations

The proliferation of desk calculators, as well as the growing use of the computer, has made most hand calculations concerning municipal bonds obsolete. Desk calculators will compute bond yields and prices in a matter of seconds. The machines can handle virtually any combination of yield or price and time to maturity. Traditionally municipal bond calculations are made on the basis of twelve months of thirty days each and 360-day years.

Most major dealers either have their own computer programs or access to outside computer companies to make calculations on bids for offerings. Once a laborious process, the calculation of the bid is now almost instantaneous. The growth of more complicated types of issues, such as housing issues and advance refundings, has required still more complex calculations. The flow of funds in these issues, and the rates at which they are invested, are very important in pricing the bonds. Again, sophisticated computer programs have been developed for the more intricate issues.

But the concepts behind these calculations are very important. The market value of a bond simply cannot be understood without a thorough grounding in how yields and prices are calculated. The value of a bid, similarly, cannot be understood without such fundamental principles.

Present Value Theory

The most important concept underlying most bond calculations is discounted present value. It is a way to take into account the time value of money. One dollar received today is worth more than one dollar tomorrow and a lot more than one dollar received ten years from now. The compound interest formula follows.

$$\text{Future value} = (1+k)^n$$

The annual interest rate is k. The number of years the investment is being held is n. The investor would earn $1+k$ in the first year. That would be reinvested and earn interest in the second year at the same rate. The total at the end of the second year is arrived at by multiplying $(1+k)$ times $(1+k)$. In the third year, the investor has a total of $(1+k)^3$, and so on. With k equal to 6%, and the investment held for ten years, the formula looks as follows.

$$\text{Future value} = (1 + .06)^{10} = 1.79$$

Finding the present value is the reverse of finding the future value. What would an investor pay today for the promise of one dollar to be paid in ten years? That depends at what rate money could be invested. Assuming it could be invested at a 6% rate of interest, the value today of one dollar received ten years from now is 56¢. This is known as the present value. The 6% rate is known as the discount rate. In other words, if an investor put 56¢ in a bank account that pays 6% compounded annually (which means that interest is paid and reinvested once a year), he or she will have one dollar at the end of ten years.

The equation to solve for present value is the inverse of the compound interest equation.

$$\text{Present value} = \frac{1}{(1+k)^n}$$

To find the present value of one dollar received ten years from now, we must assume a discount rate. For the above example, it is 6%.

$$PV = \frac{1}{(1+.06)^{10}} = \frac{1}{1.79} = .56 = 56¢$$

THE INTERNAL RATE OF RETURN

Present value theory is used in another important way. A borrower might offer a lender one dollar seven years from now in return for a loan of 75¢ today. Alternatively, another borrower might offer one dollar in six years for 85¢ today. How does the lender compare the offers? The so-called internal rate of return must be calculated for each offer. What annual return will the investor earn if he or she puts 75¢ in the equivalent of a savings account today and withdraws one dollar in seven years? The answer is about 4%. It is the internal rate of return, interest compounded annually, of the first offer. What annual rate of return will be earned on 85¢ with a payoff of one dollar in six years? The answer is about 3%. Clearly, the first offer is better, provided the investor does not mind keeping his money tied up for another year.

The internal rate of return cannot be computed as cleanly as the present value can. There is no algebraic formula for it. Instead, it is found by a trial-and-error search through the present value tables, a process now made instantaneous by computers and calculators. These readily available tables are compilations of the present values for a range of discount rates and maturities. An excerpt is shown in Figure A-1.

When the present value and maturity are known, the tables can be scanned for the appropriate rate of return. Although the computer will do the work, it is important to understand the process. In the lending example above, the 75¢ the lender would have to give up today is the present value. The maturity or duration of the loan is seven years. The question is what discount rate—internal rate of return—would make one dollar received in seven years equal to 75¢ The answer is found in the seven-year row of the present value table. Run across the seven-year row to .75, or, for the sake of simplicity, the closest value to .75, which in this case is .7599. Look up the column to see what the internal rate of return is. It is 4%. To put it another way, 75¢ (75.99¢, more precisely), invested in a savings account paying 4% a year, compounded annually, would be worth one dollar at the end of seven years. A very precise answer can be found by interpolating, as explained in a later section.

Yield to Maturity

Given the coupon, current price and time to maturity, the yield to maturity is the internal rate of return an investor earns from payments of bond interest and principal, with interest compounded semiannually. The price of the bond is precisely the present value of all the cash flows—interest and principal—discounted by the yield to maturity.

As with the concept of the internal rate of return, the yield to maturity takes into account the time value of money. The current yield

FIGURE A-1. Excerpt from Present Value Table

SCAN TABLES

PRESENT WORTH OF 1

ANNUAL COMPOUNDING

Description: This table shows what $1 to be paid in the future is worth today. Present Worth is the value today of a single payment tomorrow. Interest is computed and compounded annually.

Example: A note promising to pay $10,000 in 5 years is discounted. The discounted value of the note is $8,219.27 at a 4% rate of interest, computed and compounded annually.

YEAR	4.00 %	4.25 %	4.50 %	4.75 %	5.00 %	5.25 %	5.50 %	5.75 %
1	0.961538	0.959233	0.956938	0.954654	0.952381	0.950119	0.947867	0.945626
2	0.924556	0.920127	0.915730	0.911364	0.907029	0.902726	0.898452	0.894209
3	0.888996	0.882616	0.876297	0.870037	0.863838	0.857697	0.851614	0.845588
4	0.854804	0.846634	0.838561	0.830585	0.822702	0.814914	0.807217	0.799611
5	0.821927	0.812119	0.802451	0.792921	0.783526	0.774265	0.765134	0.756133
6	0.790315	0.779011	0.767896	0.756965	0.746215	0.735643	0.725246	0.715019
7	0.759918	0.747253	0.734828	0.722640	0.710681	0.698949	0.687437	0.676141
8	0.730690	0.716789	0.703185	0.689871	0.676839	0.664084	0.651599	0.639377
9	0.702587	0.687568	0.672904	0.658588	0.644609	0.630959	0.617629	0.604612
10	0.675564	0.659937	0.643928	0.628723	0.613913	0.599486	0.585431	0.571737
11	0.649581	0.632650	0.616199	0.600213	0.584679	0.569583	0.554911	0.540650
12	0.624597	0.606858	0.589664	0.572996	0.556837	0.541171	0.525982	0.511253
13	0.600574	0.582118	0.564272	0.547013	0.530321	0.514177	0.498561	0.483454
14	0.577475	0.558387	0.539973	0.522208	0.505068	0.488529	0.472569	0.457167
15	0.555265	0.535623	0.516720	0.498528	0.481017	0.464161	0.447933	0.432309
16	0.533908	0.513787	0.494469	0.475922	0.458112	0.441008	0.424581	0.408803
17	0.513373	0.492841	0.473176	0.454341	0.436297	0.419010	0.402447	0.386575
18	0.493628	0.472749	0.452800	0.433738	0.415521	0.398109	0.381466	0.365555
19	0.474642	0.453477	0.433302	0.414070	0.395734	0.378251	0.361579	0.345679
20	0.456387	0.434989	0.414643	0.395293	0.376889	0.359383	0.342729	0.326883
21	0.438834	0.417256	0.396787	0.377368	0.358942	0.341457	0.324862	0.309109
22	0.421955	0.400246	0.379701	0.360256	0.341850	0.324425	0.307926	0.292302
23	0.405726	0.383929	0.363350	0.343920	0.325571	0.308242	0.291873	0.276408
24	0.390121	0.368277	0.347703	0.328324	0.310068	0.292866	0.276657	0.261379
25	0.375117	0.353263	0.332731	0.313436	0.295303	0.278258	0.262234	0.247167
26	0.360689	0.338862	0.318402	0.299223	0.281241	0.264378	0.248563	0.233728
27	0.346817	0.325047	0.304691	0.285655	0.267848	0.251190	0.235605	0.221019
28	0.333477	0.311796	0.291571	0.272701	0.255094	0.238661	0.223322	0.209002
29	0.320651	0.299085	0.279015	0.260335	0.242946	0.226756	0.211679	0.197637
30	0.308319	0.286892	0.267000	0.248530	0.231377	0.215445	0.200644	0.186891

SOURCE: The Thorndike Encyclopedia of Banking and Financial Tables

does not. It is simply the annual coupon payment divided by the current price of the bond. A bond with a 6% coupon selling for 90 has a current yield of 6.67%.

$$\frac{\$60}{\$900} \text{ or } \frac{.06}{.90} = .0667$$

The current yield does not take into account the gain or loss to the investor when the bonds are redeemed, either. In the case of the discount bond above, the investor will receive $100 above the purchase price at maturity. One way to include this in the calculation would be to amortize the discount of $100 over the ten-year life of the bond on a straight-line basis. This would come to $10 a year. But it is a misleading calculation because the investor does not have use of the $100 over ten years. The yield to maturity does account for both the timing and amount of interest and principal payments. To use the savings account analogy again, it is the annual rate of return the investor would earn if he or she put the $900 paid for the bond into a savings account, received a check every six months that represented semiannual interest payments of $30, and withdrew $1,000 at the end of ten years. The answer is easily found with a bond calculator and almost as easily in the basis books published by the Financial Publishing Co., in Boston. As with any internal rate of return, there is no direct algebraic formula to compute yield to maturity. The answer is approximately 7.50%, as can be seen in Figure A-2.

The yield to maturity on a premium bond is handled similarly. A 6% ten-year bond bought at 110 has a lower yield to maturity than current yield. The investor paid $1,100 for the bond and will receive only $1,000 back if it is held to maturity. The current yield is 5.45%. Again, the premium could be amortized on a straight-line basis, reducing each interest payment for the sake of computation by $10 a year. But that distorts the true picture. The yield to maturity is the internal rate of return that an investment of $1,100 is earning from semiannual interest payments of $30 and a return of principal in ten years of $1,000. The answer is about 4.75%.

To repeat, yield to maturity calculations for most bonds assume that interest is being compounded semiannually. Also, interest paid is assumed to be reinvested at the same rate for all present value-type calculations. If an investor knows that this will not be the case, adjustments can and should be made to the calculations to get a truer internal rate of return.

FIGURE A-2. Excerpt from Basis Book

Yield	8-3	8-6	8-9	9-0	9-3	9-6	9-9	10-0
4.00	113.93	114.29	114.64	114.99	115.33	115.68	116.01	116.35
4.20	112.43	112.76	113.06	113.37	113.67	113.98	114.27	114.58
4.40	110.96	111.24	111.51	111.79	112.04	112.31	112.57	112.83
4.60	109.51	109.76	109.98	110.22	110.44	110.68	110.89	111.12
4.80	108.09	108.30	108.48	108.69	108.87	109.07	109.25	109.44
5.00	106.68	106.86	107.01	107.18	107.32	107.49	107.63	107.79
5.20	105.30	105.44	105.56	105.69	105.81	105.94	106.05	106.18
5.40	103.94	104.05	104.13	104.23	104.31	104.41	104.49	104.59
5.60	102.60	102.68	102.73	102.80	102.85	102.92	102.96	103.03
5.80	101.29	101.33	101.35	101.39	101.41	101.45	101.46	101.50
6.00	99.99	100.00	99.99	100.00	99.99	100.00	99.99	100.00
6.10	99.35	99.34	99.32	99.32	99.32	99.29	99.26	99.26
6.20	98.71	98.69	98.65	98.64	98.60	98.58	98.54	98.53
6.30	98.08	98.05	97.99	97.96	97.91	97.88	97.83	97.80
6.40	97.45	97.41	97.34	97.30	97.23	97.19	97.12	97.08
6.50	96.83	96.77	96.69	96.63	96.55	96.50	96.42	96.37
6.60	96.22	96.14	96.05	95.98	95.88	95.81	95.72	95.66
6.70	95.61	95.52	95.41	95.33	95.22	95.14	95.03	94.96
6.80	95.00	94.90	94.78	94.68	94.56	94.47	94.35	94.26
6.90	94.40	94.28	94.15	94.04	93.91	93.80	93.68	93.58
7.00	93.80	93.67	93.53	93.41	93.26	93.15	93.01	92.89
7.10	93.21	93.07	92.91	92.78	92.62	92.49	92.34	92.22
7.20	92.62	92.47	92.30	92.15	91.98	91.84	91.68	91.55
7.30	92.03	91.87	91.69	91.53	91.35	91.20	91.03	90.89
7.40	91.46	91.28	91.09	90.92	90.73	90.57	90.38	90.23 ⬅
7.50	90.88	90.70	90.49	90.31	90.11	89.94	89.74	89.58
7.60	90.31	90.11	89.89	89.71	89.49	89.31	89.11	88.93
7.70	89.75	89.54	89.31	89.11	88.88	88.69	88.48	88.29
7.80	89.18	88.97	88.72	88.51	88.28	88.08	87.85	87.66
7.90	88.63	88.40	88.14	87.92	87.68	87.47	87.23	87.03
8.00	88.07	87.83	87.57	87.34	87.09	86.87	86.62	86.41
8.10	87.53	87.28	87.00	86.76	86.50	86.27	86.01	85.79
8.20	86.98	86.72	86.44	86.19	85.91	85.67	85.41	85.18
8.30	86.44	86.17	85.88	85.62	85.33	85.09	84.81	84.58
8.40	85.90	85.63	85.32	85.05	84.76	84.50	84.22	83.98
8.50	85.37	85.08	84.77	84.49	84.19	83.93	83.64	83.38
8.60	84.84	84.55	84.22	83.94	83.63	83.35	83.05	82.79
8.70	84.32	84.01	83.68	83.39	83.07	82.78	82.48	82.21
8.80	83.80	83.48	83.14	82.84	82.51	82.22	81.91	81.63
8.90	83.29	82.96	82.61	82.30	81.96	81.66	81.34	81.06
9.00	82.77	82.44	82.08	81.76	81.41	81.11	80.78	80.49
9.10	82.27	81.92	81.55	81.23	80.87	80.56	80.22	79.92
9.20	81.76	81.41	81.03	80.70	80.34	80.02	79.67	79.37
9.30	81.26	80.90	80.52	80.17	79.80	79.48	79.12	78.81
9.40	80.76	80.40	80.00	79.65	79.28	78.94	78.58	78.26
9.50	80.27	79.90	79.50	79.14	78.75	78.41	78.05	77.72
9.60	79.78	79.40	78.99	78.63	78.23	77.89	77.51	77.18
9.70	79.30	78.91	78.49	78.12	77.72	77.37	76.99	76.65
9.80	78.82	78.42	77.99	77.62	77.21	76.85	76.46	76.12
9.90	78.34	77.93	77.50	77.12	76.70	76.34	75.94	75.60
10.00	77.86	77.45	77.01	76.62	76.20	75.83	75.43	75.08
10.20	76.93	76.50	76.05	75.64	75.21	74.83	74.41	74.05
10.40	76.00	75.56	75.10	74.68	74.24	73.84	73.42	73.04
10.60	75.09	74.64	74.16	73.73	73.28	72.87	72.44	72.05
10.80	74.20	73.73	73.24	72.80	72.33	71.92	71.47	71.08
11.00	73.31	72.84	72.34	71.88	71.41	70.98	70.53	70.12
11.20	72.45	71.96	71.44	70.98	70.49	70.06	69.60	69.19
11.40	71.59	71.09	70.57	70.10	69.60	69.15	68.68	68.26
11.60	70.75	70.24	69.70	69.22	68.71	68.26	67.78	67.36
11.80	69.91	69.40	68.85	68.36	67.85	67.39	66.90	66.47
12.00	69.10	68.57	68.01	67.52	66.99	66.53	66.03	65.59

SOURCE: Reproduced from Publication No. 83, *Expanded Bond Values Tables*, Copyright 1970, Page 589, Financial Publishing Company, Boston Massachusetts.

Calculating the Yield to Maturity

To understand fully just how the yield to maturity is calculated, it is necessary to demonstrate how the price of a bond is found when the yield to maturity is known. Municipal bonds are generally quoted in terms of yield to maturity. The investor or dealer then can derive the price of the bond. The price of a bond is precisely the sum of the present values of the cash flows—interest and principal—discounted by the yield to maturity. For example, if a bond quoted at a 7% yield to maturity has a coupon of 6% and is due in three years, the price will be the sum of the present values of each semiannual interest payment of $30, plus the present value of $1,000 received in three years, all discounted by 7%. In other words, what would an investor have to put up now to earn a 7% annual return, compounded semiannually, from interest of $30 received every six months and return of principal of $1,000 in three years? The problem can be formulated as follows.

Time from the Purchase	*Cash Received*	*Present Value at a Discount Rate of 7%*
6 months	$30.00	$28.99
12 months	30.00	28.01
18 months	30.00	27.01
24 months	30.00	26.14
30 months	30.00	25.26
36 months	1,030.00	837.91
Total	$1,180.00	$973.32

The total cash payments come to $1,180. But the sum of the present values—which is the price of the bond—is only 973.32.

Bond calculators will compute prices. Knowing the yield to maturity, coupon and time to maturity, one can also merely look for the right price in a basis book. As shown in the short excerpted page from the basis book in Figure A-3, the price, $973.40, is the same as the sum of the present values found above, except for errors due to rounding.

To find the yield to maturity when the price is known is simply the reverse of this process. The price of the bond is the present value of all future payments. In the above example, had the price of 97.34 been known, the yield to maturity would be found by hunting for the discount rate that would produce a sum of present values equal to 973.40.

FIGURE A-3. Excerpt from Basis Book

6%   YEARS and MONTHS

Yield	2-9	2-10	2-11	3-0	3-1	3-2	3-3	3-4
4.00	105.15	105.30	105.45	105.60	105.74	105.89	106.03	106.18
4.20	104.62	104.75	104.89	105.02	105.15	105.28	105.41	105.54
4.40	104.09	104.21	104.33	104.45	104.56	104.67	104.79	104.90
4.60	103.57	103.67	103.78	103.88	103.98	104.07	104.17	104.27
4.80	103.05	103.14	103.23	103.32	103.40	103.48	103.56	103.65
5.00	102.53	102.60	102.68	102.75	102.82	102.89	102.96	103.03
5.20	102.02	102.07	102.13	102.20	102.25	102.30	102.35	102.41
5.40	101.50	101.55	101.59	101.64	101.68	101.72	101.76	101.80
5.60	101.00	101.03	101.06	101.09	101.11	101.14	101.16	101.19
5.80	100.49	100.51	100.52	100.54	100.55	100.56	100.57	100.59
6.00	99.99	99.99	99.99	100.00	99.99	99.99	99.99	99.99
6.10	99.74	99.73	99.73	99.73	99.72	99.71	99.70	99.69
6.20	99.49	99.48	99.47	99.46	99.44	99.42	99.41	99.40
6.30	99.24	99.22	99.21	99.19	99.16	99.14	99.10	99.10
6.40	98.99	98.97	98.94	98.92	98.89	98.86	98.83	98.81
6.50	98.75	98.71	98.68	98.66	98.62	98.58	98.54	98.51
6.60	98.50	98.46	98.42	98.39	98.34	98.30	98.26	98.22
6.70	98.26	98.21	98.17	98.13	98.07	98.02	97.97	97.93
6.80	98.01	97.96	97.91	97.86	97.80	97.74	97.69	97.64
6.90	97.77	97.71	97.65	97.60	97.53	97.47	97.41	97.35
7.00	97.52	97.46	97.40	97.34	97.26	97.19	97.12	97.06
7.10	97.28	97.21	97.14	97.07	96.99	96.92	96.84	96.77
7.20	97.04	96.96	96.89	96.81	96.73	96.64	96.56	96.49
7.30	96.80	96.71	96.63	96.55	96.46	96.37	96.28	96.20
7.40	96.56	96.47	96.38	96.29	96.19	96.10	96.01	95.92
7.50	96.32	96.22	96.13	96.04	95.93	95.83	95.73	95.64
7.60	96.08	95.98	95.88	95.78	95.67	95.56	95.45	95.35
7.70	95.84	95.73	95.63	95.52	95.40	95.29	95.18	95.07
7.80	95.61	95.49	95.38	95.27	95.14	95.02	94.90	94.79
7.90	95.37	95.25	95.13	95.01	94.88	94.75	94.63	94.51
8.00	95.13	95.00	94.88	94.76	94.62	94.49	94.36	94.23
8.10	94.90	94.76	94.63	94.50	94.36	94.22	94.09	93.96
8.20	94.67	94.52	94.39	94.25	94.10	93.96	93.82	93.68
8.30	94.43	94.28	94.14	94.00	93.85	93.69	93.55	93.41
8.40	94.20	94.04	93.90	93.75	93.59	93.43	93.28	93.13
8.50	93.97	93.81	93.65	93.50	93.33	93.17	93.01	92.86
8.60	93.74	93.57	93.41	93.25	93.08	92.91	92.75	92.59
8.70	93.50	93.33	93.17	93.00	92.82	92.65	92.48	92.32
8.80	93.27	93.10	92.92	92.76	92.57	92.39	92.22	92.05
8.90	93.04	92.86	92.68	92.51	92.32	92.13	91.95	91.78
9.00	92.82	92.63	92.44	92.26	92.07	91.88	91.69	91.51
9.10	92.59	92.39	92.20	92.02	91.82	91.62	91.43	91.24
9.20	92.36	92.16	91.96	91.77	91.57	91.36	91.17	90.97
9.30	92.13	91.93	91.73	91.53	91.32	91.11	90.91	90.71
9.40	91.91	91.70	91.49	91.29	91.07	90.86	90.65	90.44
9.50	91.68	91.47	91.25	91.05	90.82	90.60	90.39	90.18
9.60	91.46	91.24	91.02	90.81	90.57	90.35	90.13	89.92
9.70	91.23	91.01	90.78	90.56	90.33	90.10	89.88	89.66
9.80	91.01	90.78	90.55	90.33	90.08	89.85	89.62	89.40
9.90	90.79	90.55	90.31	90.09	89.84	89.60	89.36	89.14
10.00	90.57	90.32	90.08	89.85	89.60	89.35	89.11	88.88
10.20	90.13	89.87	89.62	89.38	89.11	88.86	88.61	88.36
10.40	89.69	89.42	89.16	88.90	88.63	88.36	88.10	87.85
10.60	89.25	88.97	88.70	88.44	88.15	87.88	87.61	87.34
10.80	88.82	88.53	88.25	87.97	87.68	87.39	87.11	86.84
11.00	88.39	88.09	87.80	87.51	87.21	86.91	86.62	86.34
11.20	87.96	87.65	87.35	87.05	86.74	86.43	86.13	85.84
11.40	87.53	87.21	86.90	86.60	86.27	85.96	85.65	85.35
11.60	87.11	86.78	86.46	86.14	85.81	85.48	85.17	84.86
11.80	86.69	86.35	86.02	85.69	85.35	85.02	84.69	84.37
12.00	86.27	85.92	85.58	85.25	84.90	84.55	84.21	83.89

SOURCE: Reproduced from Publication No. 83, *Expanded Bond Values Tables,* Copyright 1970, page 584, Financial Publishing Company, Boston, Massachusetts.

As pointed out in the section on internal rate of return, a trial-and-error search is unavoidable if computed by hand. For a 6% ten-year bond bought at 90, the present value of all future cash flows must come to 900. To find the yield to maturity, a discount rate would have to be applied to each semiannual payment to derive the present value. If the sum of these present values did not equal 900, another rate would be tried, and so on.

Interpolation

Before the sophisticated desk calculator, the basis book was an essential tool for all professionals in the municipal bond industry. In practicality, however, no matter how detailed the basis book, all permutations are not recorded. Basis books typically record the values for bonds with increments in yields of .05%. Occasionally, municipal bonds are quoted in increments of ⅛ of 1%, or other odd rates. Maturities are usually broken down on a monthly basis. But most frequently, a bond will have an odd number of days to maturity.

Interpolation is used to compute prices and yields for bonds that fall between the proverbial cracks of the basis book. (Calculators can generally compute values of bonds with odd terms.) For small increments, there is very close to a constant linear relationship between yields to maturity and prices. By taking an average or proportion between two values in a bond table, the exact yield or price can be approximated very closely.

For example, a 5% bond yielding 4.00% to maturity is due in ten years and three months. The bond table shows that the price for a bond due in exactly ten years is 108.18. The price of a bond due in ten years and six months is 108.51. A bond due in ten years and three months would fall precisely between those two prices. Simply take the sum of the two, which equals 216.69. Then divide by two. The answer is 108.35.

Calculations can be made for maturities with an odd number of days by taking the proportion of those days to the period for where there are values in the bond table. If the bonds were due in ten years and 20 days, price or yield would lie between the ten-year and ten-year-six-month values in a proportion of 20 to 180. Remember, in municipal bond calculations, all months have thirty days. Similarly, the prices of bonds with odd yields can be found by interpolating between the given values.

Yield to Call

Most municipal bonds are issued with call provisions. This feature gives the issuer the right to redeem the bonds after a specified period of time at a specified price. The yield to call measures the yield (internal rate of return) that would be earned if the bonds were called at the call price. Typically, dealers will quote both the yield to maturity and the yield to call to investors if the yield to call is lower. In written confirmations of orders, the Municipal Securities Rulemaking Board requires that the yield to call be stated if it is lower than the yield to maturity.

A typical call provision allows the issuer to redeem the bonds ten years after they are issued at a price of 103. The yield is calculated in the same way as the yield to maturity except that the redemption price is $1,030 and the time to maturity is ten years. With such a call provision, a 6%, 20-year bond would have a yield to call of 6.22%. If the above bond had been bought at the end of the fifth year at 105, its yield to call would be only 5.35% Its yield to maturity at the same time would be 5.50%.

Capital Gains Taxes

An adjustment to yield to maturity must be made for bonds bought below par because the discount is subject to capital gains taxes. The taxes must be deducted from the principal in computing the after-tax yield to maturity. It is generally difficult for an investor to know precisely what the capital gains tax will be when the bonds are due. The maximum tax on long-term gains is 20%. Many dealers construct tables assuming a capital gains reduction of 20% on the discount.

A 6% bond bought at 90 and due in 20 years would be subject to capital gains taxes. Assuming a capital gains rate of 20%, the $100 gain at maturity would be reduced by 20% or $20. The yield to maturity, then, would be computed by assuming the investor would get back $980 rather than the full $1,000. The yield to maturity, at a 20% capital gains tax, is 6.88%. Without capital gains tax, the yield to maturity would be 6.93%. The tax consequences of premium bonds are discussed in Chapter 7.

Discount Notes

Treasury bills and other short-term government securities, as well as commercial paper, are usually issued on a discounted basis. The certificate does not bear interest—that is, traditional interest payments are not made. Rather, the security is issued at a discount and then paid in full at maturity. The difference between the purchase price and the value at maturity is, in effect, the interest earned.

Occasionally, short-term tax-exempt notes are issued on a discounted basis, although the practice has become rare. Computation of the interest earned is straightforward. It is the amount of the discount divided by the amount paid for the security. A $1,000 one-year note issued at $950 has a discount of $50. The investor will receive the full $1,000 in one year. The actual interest income earned equals $50/$950, or 5.26%. Note that the interest is always slightly more than the percentage amount of the discount because the investor is putting up less than the full amount that will be paid back.

Calculating the Bid

Computing the interest cost on a new issue generally is not a simple matter. The issuer must be able to determine which bid by competing syndicates produces a lower interest cost. This would obviously be quite straightforward for an issue with all bonds maturing at one date. The lower the coupon rate on such an issue, the lower the interest cost to the issuer, provided the bonds are not issued at a premium or discount.

But because municipal bonds are generally issued in serial maturities, the determination of the total interest cost can be quite complex. To deal with this problem, the industry developed a simplifying formula that ignores the time value of money in measuring interest costs. The computation, known as the net interest cost (NIC), can be calculated relatively quickly by hand. And the NIC has continued as the primary method of submitting bids, although computers have made more complex methods just as easy to compute. NIC is a way to measure the total amount of interest, without regard for the time value of money that will be paid over the life of an issue.

With the growing use of the computer, a method of determining the interest cost that does account for the time value of interest payments has been growing in use. The measure is called true interest cost, or TIC.

Returning to present value theory, TIC is the internal rate of return that will be paid by the issuer to investors. It is that discount rate that will equalize the sum of the present values of the issuer's cash payments to the bond proceeds collected by the issuer when the bonds are issued. This will be explained more fully below, but it is important to note that TIC and NIC can be significantly different for the same offering.

NET INTEREST COST

NIC is derived by adding the total volume of interest payments for the entire offering and dividing by the amount of bonds outstanding times the years they are outstanding. If the bonds were issued at a discount, the amount of the discount is added to the interest payments as if it were an outlay by the issuer. If the bonds were issued at a premium, the amount would be subtracted from interest payments. The formula is as follows:

$$NIC = \frac{\text{total interest payments} + \text{discount (or} - \text{premium)}}{\text{bond year dollars}}$$

Bond year dollars measure the amount of bonds outstanding over the time they are outstanding—in other words, how much is outstanding for how long. Bond years alone are simply the number of bonds outstanding (in $1,000 denominations) times the number of years they are outstanding. One bond year is one $1,000 bond outstanding for one year. Bond year dollars are the number of bond years multiplied by $1,000 for each bond.

The Center for Capital Market Research at the University of Oregon, which has done a great deal of research into these methods, provides the following example of the NIC calculation. The NIC is computed for a $3,000 offering with three serial maturities and a constant coupon of 5% for each maturity.

EXAMPLE 1

Years to Maturity	Par Value	Coupon Rate	Coupon Payments per Maturity	Bond Year Dollars
1	$1,000	5%	$ 50	$1,000
2	1,000	5	100	2,000
3	1,000	5	150	3,000
Total	$3,000		$300	$6,000

The total interest payments come to $300. $50 is paid out for the first maturity, which is due in a year. $50 a year is paid out for two years on the second maturity, and for three years on the third maturity. The bonds were issued at par so there is no addition or deduction from the total interest payments for a discount or premium. Bond year dollars equal $6,000. The NIC equals 5%.

$$NIC = \frac{\text{Total coupon payments}}{\text{Bond year dollars}} = \frac{\$300}{\$6,000} = .05 = 5\%$$

Because the coupon rate was the same for all three issues, the NIC was precisely equal to the coupon rate. A somewhat more complicated example will help make the calculation clearer. An issuer chooses to sell $10,000 of bonds in five separate maturities. The serial maturities and the coupon rates follow. There are no discounts or premiums.

EXAMPLE 2

Years to Maturity	Par Value	Coupon Rate
1	$1,000	5.00%
2	2,000	5.10
3	2,000	5.20
4	2,000	5.25
5	3,000	5.30

The total interest payments and bond year dollars follow, in order of maturity.

Coupon Payments per Maturity	Bond Year Dollars
$ 50	$ 1,000
204	4,000
312	6,000
420	8,000
795	15,000
TOTAL $1,781	$34,000

$$NIC = \frac{\text{Total interest}}{\text{Bond year dollars}} = \frac{\$1,781}{\$34,000} = .05238 = 5.24\%$$

Had the issue been sold at a discount, the NIC would be higher. If the issue had sold at an average price of, say, 97, the issuer would have had $300 less in proceeds. To compute the NIC, the $300 would be added to total interest payments. The NIC rises to 6.12%.

$$\text{NIC} = \frac{\$1,781 + 300}{\$34,000} = \frac{\$\,2,081}{\$34,000} = .06121 = 6.12\%$$

TRUE INTEREST COST

There are a growing number of critics of NIC. They argue that because the method entirely ignores the timing of interest payments, it can often mislead an issuer into choosing a bid with a higher cost to the issuer. In the previous example, the NIC was a function only of the total amount of interest, and did not take into account the consideration of when the interest payments were made. In other words, all $1,781 of interest could have been paid in the first year and the NIC would have still equaled 5.24%.

TIC does account for the time value of money. The underlying theory is the same as that which supports the yield to maturity. TIC is the yearly interest rate an issuer would be paying if it were a bank whose savers deposited the bond proceeds and withdrew the interest and principal according to the maturity schedule.

The TIC for Example 2 is not significantly different from the NIC, but a look at how it is computed is valuable. The TIC is 5.236%. The NIC is 5.238%.

Time to Maturity (Months)	Total Interest Paid	+	Principal Paid	Present Value of Cash Flow Discounted By 5.236%
6	$ 260.00			$ 253.37
12	260.00		$ 1,000.00	1,196.53
18	235.00			217.47
24	235.00		2,000.00	2,015.50
30	184.00			161.70
36	184.00		2,000.00	1,870.30
42	132.00			110.15
48	132.00		2,000.00	1,733.80
54	79.50			63.00
60	79.50		3,000.00	2,378.18
TOTAL	$ 1,781.00		$10,000.00	$10,000.00

The TIC is the rate that will discount all future cash payments so that the sum of their present value equals the bond proceeds. Note that the sum of the present value of all the cash flows equals $10,000 when discounted at 5.236%. Interest is assumed to be compounded semi-annually. If the offering has been issued at 97, the TIC would have differed more sharply from the NIC. The bond proceeds would have equaled $9,700. The TIC that would discount the present values to equal $9,700 is 6.24%. The NIC for the issue at discount would have been 6.12%.

Because there is no algebraic formula, the TIC can only be found with a search through the present value tables. The best way to start out is by computing the NIC. Then a yield slightly above or below the NIC can be tried out to discount the cash flows to their present value. If the sum of the present values is too high, a higher discount rate must be tried. If the sum is less than the proceeds, a lower rate is tried. After many attempts, the final yield can be zeroed in on.

Computers can calculate such bids almost instantaneously. The information is fed into a computer program, which, in effect, searches for the right answer in much the same way it would be done by hand. The spreading use of the computer has enabled issuers to demand TIC as a basis for assessing bids more frequently.

Differences Between NIC and TIC

The Center for Capital Market Research of the University of Oregon has prepared several examples to show how NIC and TIC can be significantly different. The problem with NIC is that it does not account for the time value of interest payments. As we discussed earlier, the NIC would not change, whether all the interest payments were made in the first year or the last year. Before TIC a few issues were structured with high coupons for early maturities, offset by low coupons on later ones. The net effect is to lower NIC, although such a structure would usually result in a higher TIC.

Again, the reason this works is that NIC ignores the time value of interest payments. Higher coupons on early maturities result in higher bond prices. But to get the same price premium on a short-term bond as a long-term bond requires a lower total interest payment. Likewise, for every dollar of interest paid over the life of a bond, one would get a higher price on short-term securities than on longer-term securities. The yield to maturity calculations do take the time value of money into account.

An example will help clarify this principle. A one-year bond with an 8% coupon would be priced at 100.95 to yield 7% to maturity. A ten-year bond with an 8% coupon would be priced at 107.11 to yield 7% annually. The $10 of extra interest paid on the one-year bond results in a price premium of $9.50, or 95¢ for every dollar of interest paid in excess of what would have been paid if the bond were priced at par. On the ten-year bond, a total of $100 in extra interest is paid over the life of the bond. The premium paid is $71.11, or only 71¢ per dollar of interest paid in excess of what would have been paid if the bond were priced to sell at par.

Because NIC will be minimized if the dollar amount of interest paid is minimized while the price of the securities is maximized, some under-writers use the "high-low" technique to price offerings. When taking the time value of money into account, however, the higher coupons on early maturities do penalize the issuer who must pay out the money sooner than would otherwise be necessary. TIC reflects this. It rises if the bulk of interest is paid early and falls if interest payments are pushed back.

The Center for Capital Market Research provides a couple of simple examples based on Example 1 that illustrate this important point. For both the following issues, interest payments equal $300 and total debt service equals $3,300. The NIC for both issues is 5%. But the TIC for Issue A is 5.04% because coupon payments are made earlier. The TIC for Issue B is only 4.98% because interest payments are made later.

		Issue A NIC = 5% TIC = 5.04%		Issue B NIC = 5% TIC = 4.98%	
Years to Maturity	Par Value	Coupon Rate	Annual Debt Service	Coupon Rate	Annual Debt Service
1	$1,000	12%	$1,190	2%	$1,130
2	1,000	3	1,070	5	1,110
3	1,000	4	1,040	6	1,060
TOTAL	$3,000		$3,300		$3,300

In addition, economists at the University of Oregon argue that high- and low-coupon bonds that are otherwise equivalent will often trade at higher yields to maturity than bonds priced closer to par. This penalty yield arises for several reasons. Traders say that bonds with high premiums are relatively rare and the market is unfamiliar with them. There is also more coupon to be reinvested, which increases the risk and transaction cost of reinvestment. Similarly, discount bonds will also sell at comparatively higher yields, largely because the discount is subject to capital gains tax. Bids with high- and low-coupons are often inefficient, says the Center, and result in a higher total interest cost to the issuer.

The Center for Capital Market Research has constructed a set of restrictions that will bring the NIC more closely in line with the TIC. Among the most common of these is for the issuer to place a maximum limit on the coupon rate to avoid bonds with large premiums in the early years. A maximum limit can also be placed on the size of any discount that the issue is sold for. A discount is just like a coupon payment at the beginning of the issue. One other popular restriction is to require that coupon rates on succeeding maturities are equal to or higher than the rate on the preceding maturity. This keeps underwriters from front-loading the issue with heavy coupon payments. See the Center's publication "Improving Bidding Rules to Reduce Interest Costs in the Competitive Sale of Municipal Bonds" for a complete discussion of bidding rules.

Average Life of Serial Bonds

The average life of a municipal bond offering is the number of bond years divided by the total number of bonds in the issue. In Example 2, the total number of bond years is 34. There are ten bonds in the $10,000 issue. The average life = 34/10 = 3.4.

Bibliography

Chapter 1

Selling Municipal Bonds, E. F. Hutton Public Finance Group, E. F. Hutton & Co., New York, 1978.

"The Federal Securities Laws and Transactions in Municipal Securities," Robert W. Doty and John E. Petersen, *Northwestern University Law Review,* July-August 1976, Vol. #3, pp. 283-416.

Municipal Finance Statistics, The Bond Buyer, New York, Annual.

Tax Exempt Securities: An Investors Guide, Public Securities Association, New York, 1979.

Comprehensive Bond Values Tables, Financial Publishing Co., Boston.

"Restoring Credit and Confidence, A Report to the New York State Moreland Act Commission," 1976.

Fundamentals of Municipal Securities, ed. by Gordon L. Calvert, Securities Industry Association, New York, 1972.

Changing Conditions in the Market for State and Local Government Debt, Joint Economic Committee, Congress of the United States, 1976.

XYZ's of Arbitrage, Frederic L. Ballard, Jr., The Packard Press, Philadelphia, 1979.

The Complete Bond Book, David M. Darst, McGraw-Hill Book Co., New York, 1975.

Chapter 2

Directory of Municipal Bond Dealers of the United States, The Bond Buyer, New York (quarterly).

Chapter 3

Pitfalls in Issuing Municipal Bonds, Moody's Investors Service, Inc., New York, 1977.

The Fiscal Outlook for Cities, ed. by Roy Bahl, Syracuse University Press, Syracuse, New York, 1978.

Administration of Local Government Debt, Lennox L. Moak, Municipal Finance Officers Association, Chicago, 1970.

Concepts and Practices in Local Government Finance, Lennox L. Moak and Albert M. Hillhouse, Municipal Finance Officers Association, Chicago, 1975.

State and Local Government Finance and Financial Management, A Compendium of Current Research, ed. by John E. Petersen, Catherine L. Spain, Martharose F. Laffey, Government Finance Research Center, Washington, D.C., 1978.

Improving Bidding Rules to Reduce Interest Costs in the Competitive Sale of Municipal Bonds: A Handbook for Municipal Finance Officers, Center for Capital Market Research, University of Oregon, Eugene, 1977.

Selling Your City: A Primer for Government Officials on Communicating with the Investment Community, Peter F. Rousmaniere, Council on Municipal Performance, 1978.

Government Accounting and Financial Reporting Principles, Statement 1, National Council on Governmental Accounting, 1979.

Disclosure Guidelines for Offerings of Securities by State and Local Governments, Municipal Finance Officers Association, Chicago, 1976.

Governmental Accounting, Auditing and Financial Reporting, National Committee on Governmental Accounting, Municipal Finance Officers Association, Chicago, 1968.

Financial Accounting in Nonbusiness Organizations, Robert N. Anthony, Financial Accounting Standards Board, Stamford, Ct., 1978.

How Cities Can Improve Their Financial Reporting, Ernst & Whinney, New York, 1979.

Chapter 4

Municipal Bond Finance and Administration, Alan Rabinowitz, John Wiley and Sons, New York, 1969.

Fundamentals of Municipal Securities, ed. by Gordon L. Calvert, Securities Industry Association, New York, 1973.

Chapter 6

Tax Exempt Unit Investment Trusts: An Investor's Guide, Public Securities Association, New York, 1978.

The Complete Bond Book, David M. Darst, McGraw-Hill Book Co., New York, 1975.

Investment Analysis and Portfolio Management, Jerome B. Cohen, Edward D. Finberg, Arthur Zeibel, Dow Jones-Irwin, Inc., Horneroad, Illinois, 1973.

Building a Broader Market, Ronald W. Forbes and John E. Petersen, McGraw-Hill Book Co., New York, 1976.

Changing Conditions in the Market for State and Local Government Debt, Joint Economic Committee, Congress of the United States, 1976.

"What Is Tax Exemption Really Worth? Including Taxable Equivalent Yield Tables: The Combined Impact of Federal, State, and Local

Tax Exemption," Toni J. Elliott and George D. Friedlander, Smith Barney, Harris Upham & Co., Incorporated, 1980.

Chapter 7

Tax Exempt Financing of Housing Investment, George E. Peterson with Brian Cooper, The Urban Institute, Washington, D.C., 1979.

City Financial Emergencies, Advisory Commission on Intergovernmental Relations, Washington, D.C., 1973.

Municipal and International Bond Ratings, Standard & Poor's Corporation, New York.

The Rating Game, John E. Petersen, Twentieth Century Fund, New York, 1974.

"Notes on the Measurement of Credit Capacity," Philip M. Dearborn, from *Local Government Debt Administration Services Handbook,* Municipal Finance Officers Association, Chicago, 1978.

"*Debt Measurement—A Comparative Study,*" Ronald W. Forbes, The First Boston Corporation, New York, 1977.

Audits of State and Local Governmental Units, American Institute of Certified Public Accountants, New York, 1975.

Projecting the Fiscal Viability of Cities, Roy Bahl and Bernard Jump, Jr. Metropolitan Studies Program, Maxwell School of Citizenship and Public Affairs, Syracuse University, 1977.

"Fundamentals of General Obligation and Revenue Bond Analysis," Bernard L. Smith, Jr., The First Boston Corporation, New York, 1976.

The Postwar Quality of State and Local Debt, George H. Hempel, National Bureau of Economic Research, New York, 1971.

Chapter 8

Prospects for the American Financial Markets in 1979, Salomon Brothers, New York.

Prospects for Capital Formation and Capital Markets, Arnold W. Sauretz, Lexington Books, Lexington, Massachusetts, 1978.

Flow of Funds, Federal Reserve Board, Washington, D.C.

Credit and Capital Markets 1979, Bankers Trust Company, New York.

Function and Analysis of Capital Market Rates, James C. Van Horne, Prentice-Hall, Inc., Englewood Cliffs, New Jersey, 1970.

Inside the Money Market, Wesley Linton, Random House, New York, 1972.

"An Empirical Analysis of the Market for Tax-Exempt Securities: Estimates and Forecasts," Patrick H. Hendershott and Timothy W. Koch, Center for the Study of Financial Institutions, New York University, 1977.

Chapter 9

Municipal Securities Rulemaking Board Manual, Laws, Rules and Regulations, Commerce Clearing House Inc., 1979.

Statement of Hawkins, Delafield & Wood, Re: Proposed Tax Reform Act of 1969, New York, 1969.

Municipal Bond Finance and Administration, Alan Rabinowitz, John Wiley and Sons, New York, 1969.

Building a Broader Market, Ronald W. Forbes and John E. Petersen, McGraw-Hill Book Co., New York, 1976.

SEC Staff Report on Transaction in Securities of the City of New York, 1977.

"Securities Law Duties of Bond Counsel," C. Richard Johnson and Robert H. Wheeler, *Duke Law Journal*, 1976, Number 6.

"Searching for Standards: Disclosure in the Municipal Securities Market," John E. Petersen, Robert W. Doty, Ronald W. Forbes, Donald D. Bourgene, *Duke Law Journal*, 1976, Number 6.

A Guide To Writing A Compliance Manual For MSRB Rules, Public Securities Association, New York, 1978.

Appendix

Standard Securities Calculation Methods, Bruce M. Spence, Jacob Y. Grandenz, John J. Lynch, Jr., Securities Industry Association, New York, 1973.

Inside the Yield Book, Sidney Homer and Martin L. Liebowitz, Prentice-Hall, Inc., and New York Institute of Finance, New York, 1977.

"Costs to Municipalities of Selling Bonds by NIC," Michael H. Hopewell and George G. Kaufman, Center for Capital Market Research, University of Oregon, Eugene, *National Tax Journal*, Vol. XXVII, March 1974.

Improving Bidding Rules to Reduce Interest Costs in the Competitive Sale of Municipal Bonds: A Handbook For Municipal Finance Officers, Center for Capital Market Research, University of Oregon, Eugene, 1977.

Glossary of Municipal Terminology

Accrued Interest—Interest earned on a security since the later of the last coupon payment date or the dated date.

Ad Valorem Tax—A tax based on the value (or assessed value) of property.

Assessed Valuation—The valuation placed on property for purposes of taxation.

Basis Point—Yields on municipal securities are usually quoted in increments of basis points. One basis point is equal to 1/100 of 1 percent.

Basis Price—The price of a security expressed in yield or percentage of return on the investment.

Bearer Security—A security that has no identification as to owner. It is presumed to be owned, therefore, by the bearer or the person who holds it. Bearer securities are freely and easily negotiable since ownership can be quickly transferred from seller to buyer.

Bond—An interest-bearing promise to pay a specified sum of money—the principal amount—due on a specific date.

Bond Anticipation Note—BANs are issued by states and municipalities to obtain interim financing for projects that will eventually be funded long term through the sale of a bond issue.

Bond Bank—Institutions established in a few states to buy entire issues of bonds of municipalities, financed by the issuance of bonds by the bond bank.

Bond Funds—Registered investment companies whose assets are invested in diversified portfolios of bonds.

Brokers—In the municipal securities market brokers play an important role in the secondary market by buying from and selling to dealers.

Callable Bonds—Bonds that are redeemable by the issuer prior to the specified maturity date at a specified price at or above par.

Competitive Underwriting—A sale of municipal securities by an issuer in which underwriters or syndicates of underwriters submit sealed bids to purchase the securities. This is contrasted with a negotiated underwriting.

Concession—The allowance (or profit) that an underwriter allows a nonmember of the account; sometimes referred to as dealer's allowance.

Confirmation—A written document confirming an oral transaction in municipal securities that provides pertinent information to the customer concerning the securities and the terms of the transaction.

Coupon—The part of a bond that denotes the amount of interest due and on what date and where the payment is to be made. Coupons are presented to the issuer's designated paying agent or deposited in a commercial bank for collection. Coupons are generally payable semiannually.

Coverage—This is a term usually connected with revenue bonds. It indicates the margin of safety for payment of debt service, reflecting the number of times by which earnings for a period of time exceed debt service payable in such period.

Current Yield—The ratio of interest to the actual market price of the bond stated as a percentage. For example, a $1,000 bond that pays $80 per year in interest would have a current yield of 8%.

CUSIP—The Committee on Uniform Security Identification Procedures, which was established under the auspices of the American Bankers Association to develop a uniform method of identifying municipal, U.S. government and corporate securities.

Dated Date—The date of a bond issue from which the bondholder is entitled to receive interest, even though the bonds may actually be delivered at some other date.

Dealer—A securities firm or department of a commercial bank that engages in the underwriting, trading and sales of municipal securities.

Debt Limit—The statutory or constitutional maximum debt that an issuer can legally incur.

Debt Service—The payments required for interest on and repayment of principal amount of debt.

Default—Failure to pay principal or interest promptly when due.

Denomination—The face amount or par value of a security that the issuer promises to pay on the maturity date. Most municipal bonds are issued in a minimum denomination of $5,000, although a few older issues are available in $1,000 denominations. Notes are generally available in a $25,000 minimum denomination.

Discount—The amount by which the purchase price of a security is less than the principal amount or par value.

Dollar Bond—A bond that is quoted and traded in dollar prices rather than in terms of yield.

Double-Barreled Bond—A bond secured by the pledge of two or more sources of repayment, such as the unlimited taxing power of the issuer as well as revenues generated by a particular user charge.

Double Exemption—Securities that are exempt from state as well as Federal income taxes are said to have double exemption.

Face Amount—The par value (i.e., principal or maturity value) of a security appearing on the face of the instrument.

Financial Advisor—A consultant to an issuer of municipal securities who provides the issuer with advice with respect to the structure, timing, terms, or other similar matters concerning a new issue of securities.

Financial and Operations Principal—A municipal securities employee who is required to meet qualifications standards established by the MSRB. The individual is the person designated to be in charge of the preparation and filing of financial reports to the SEC and other regulatory bodies.

General Obligation Bond—A bond secured by the pledge of the issuer's full faith, credit and, usually, taxing power.

Industrial Revenue Bond—A security issued by a state, certain agencies or authorities, a local government or development corporation to finance the construction or purchase of industrial plants and/or equipment to be leased to a private corporation; and backed by the credit of the private corporation rather than the credit of the issuer.

Interest—Compensation paid or to be paid for the use of money. Interest is generally expressed as an annual percentage rate.

Issuer—A state, political subdivision, agency, or authority that borrows money through the sale of bonds or notes.

Legal Opinion—An opinion concerning the validity of a securities issue with respect to statutory authority, constitutionality, procedural conformity, and usually the exemption of interest from Federal income taxes. The legal opinion is usually rendered by a law firm recognized as specializing in public borrowings, often referred to as "bond counsel."

Limited Tax Bond—A bond secured by a pledge of a tax or category of taxes limited as to rate or amount.

Marketability—A measure of the ease with which a security can be sold in the secondary market.

Maturity—The date when the principal amount of a security becomes due and payable.

Moral Obligation Bond—A type of municipal security that is not backed by the full faith and credit of a state, but state law provides that the state will replenish the issue's debt service reserve fund if necessary.

Mortgage Revenue Bond—A tax-exempt security issued by a state, certain agencies or authorities, or a local government to make or purchase loans (including mortgages or other owner-financing) with respect to single-family residences.

Municipal Securities Principal—A municipal securities employee under MSRB rules who has supervisory responsibility for the municipal securities operations of the firm.

Municipal Securities Representatives—The broadest class of municipal securities professionals required to pass a qualifications examination under the rules of the Municipal Securities Rulemaking Board. This group includes individuals who underwrite, trade or sell municipal securities, does research or offers investment advice, provides financial advisory services or communicates with investors in municipal securities.

Municipal Securities Rulemaking Board (MSRB)—An independent self-regulatory organization established by the Securities Acts Amendments of 1975, which is charged with primary rulemaking authority over dealers, dealer banks, and brokers in municipal securities. Its 15 members are divided into three categories—securities firms representatives, bank dealer representatives, and public members, each category having equal representation on the Board.

Negotiated Underwriting—In a negotiated underwriting the issuer of municipal securities chooses one underwriter or a group of underwriters to sell its bonds to investors. There is no competitive bid for the issue.

Net Direct Debt—Total direct debt of a municipality less all self-supporting debt, any sinking funds and tax anticipation notes and revenue anticipation notes.

Net Interest Cost—The traditional method of calculating bids for new issues of municipal securities. The other method is known as the True Interest Cost.

Non-Callable Bond—A bond that cannot be called either for redemption by or at the option of the issuer before its specified maturity date.

Notes—Short-term promises to pay specified amounts of money, secured by specific sources of future revenues, such as taxes, Federal and state aid payments, and bond proceeds.

Notice of Sale—An official document disseminated by an issuer of municipal securities that gives pertinent information regarding an upcoming bond issue and invites bids from prospective underwriters.

Offering Price—The price at which members of an underwriting syndicate for a new issue will offer securities to investors.

Official Statement—Document prepared by or for the issuer that gives in some detail security and financial information about the issue.

Over-the-Counter Market (OTC)—A securities market that is conducted among dealers throughout the country through negotiation rather than through the use of an auction system as represented by a stock exchange.

Overlapping Debt—That portion of the debt of other governmental units for which residents of a particular municipality are responsible (e.g., for services or facilities shared by several municipalities).

Par Value—The principal amount of a bond or note due at maturity.

Paying Agent—Place where principal and interest are payable. Usually a designated bank or the office of the treasurer of the issuer.

Pollution Control Bond—A tax-exempt security issued by a state, certain agencies or authorities, a local government or development corporation to finance the construction of air or water pollution control facilities or sewage or solid waste disposal facilities pursuant to Federal law and backed by the credit of the pollution control entity rather than the credit of the issuer.

Premium—The amount by which the price of a security exceeds its principal amount.

Primary Market (new issue market)—Market for new issues of municipal bonds and notes.

Principal—The face amount of a bond, exclusive of accrued interest and payable at maturity.

Project Notes—Short-term tax-exempt securities issued under a program of the U.S. Department of Housing and Urban Development to fund local housing and urban renewal projects that are secured by both revenues from those projects and the full faith and credit of the U.S. government.

Ratings—Designations used by investor's services to give relative indications of credit quality.

Reciprocal Immunity Doctrine—The doctrine that many legal experts believe provides the constitutional basis for the exemption from Federal taxation of the interest earned on municipal securities. The doctrine holds that the states are immune from Federal interference in their affairs, just as the Federal government is immune from state interference.

Refunding—A system by which a bond issue is redeemed by a new bond issue under conditions generally more favorable to the issuer.

Registered Bond—A bond whose owner is registered with the issuer or its agents, either as to both principal and interest or as to principal only. Transfer of ownership can be accomplished only when the securities are properly endorsed by the registered owner.

Revenue Anticipation Notes—RANs are issued in anticipation of other sources of future revenue, typically Federal or state aid.

Revenue Bond—A bond payable solely from net or gross non-tax revenues derived from tolls, charges or rents paid by users of the facility constructed with the proceeds of the bond issue.

Secondary Market—Market for issues previously offered or sold.

Serial Issue—An issue that has maturities scheduled annually or, in some cases, semiannually over a period of years.

Sinking Fund—A fund accumulated by an issuer over a period of time to be used for retirement of debt, either periodically or at one time.

Special Tax Bond—A bond secured by a special tax, such as a gasoline tax.

Spread—(1) Difference between bid and asked prices on a security. (2) Difference between yields on or prices of two securities of differing sorts or differing maturities. (3) In underwriting, difference between price realized by the issuer and price paid by the investor.

Swap—A transaction in which an investor sells one security and simultaneously buys another with the proceeds, usually for about the same price.

Syndicate—A group of investment bankers and commercial banks who buy (underwrite) a new issue from the issuer and offer it for resale to the general public.

Take-down (sometimes referred to as take-down concession)—The discount from the list price allowed to a member of an underwriting account on any bonds he sells.

Tax Anticipation Notes—TANs are issued by states or municipalities to finance current operations in anticipation of future tax receipts.

Tax Base—The total property and resources subject to taxation.

Term Issue—An issue that has a single stated maturity.

Total Bonded Debt—Total general obligation debt issued by a municipality, regardless of the purpose.

Total Direct Debt—The sum of the total bonded debt and any unfunded debt (typically short-term notes) of a municipality.

Transcript of Proceedings—Documents relating to a municipal bond issue.

True Interest Cost—A method of calculating bids for new issues of municipal securities that takes in consideration the time value of money. Also see NET INTEREST COST.

Trustee—A bank designated by the issuer as the custodian of funds and official representative of bondholders. Trustees are appointed to insure compliance with the contract and represent bondholders to enforce their contract with the issuers.

Underwrite—To purchase a bond or note issue from the issuing body to resell it to the general public.

Unit Investment Trust (Municipal)—A fixed portfolio of tax-exempt bonds sold in fractional, undivided interests (usually $1,000).

Unlimited Tax Bond—A bond secured by the pledge of taxes that are not limited by rate or amount.

Yield to Maturity—A yield concept designed to give the investor the average annual yield on a security. It is based on the assumption that the security is held to maturity and that all interest received over the life of the security can be reinvested at the yield to maturity.

Index